Ninian Smart was
Glasgow Academy
from 1945 to 194
of Oxford where
He subsequently lectu
University College of Wales and at Yale University
in the United States. He held the post of lecturer
in the History of the Philosophy of Religion at
London University, and was H. G. Wood Professor
of Theology at Birmingham University. His present
position is Professor of Religious Studies at the
University of Lancaster. He is a frequent broad-
caster, and his books include *Reasons and Faiths*
(1958), *Philosophers and Religious Truth* (1969),
and *The Religious Experience of Mankind* (1971).

MAO

Ninian Smart

FONTANA/COLLINS

First issued in Fontana 1974
© Ninian Smart 1974

Made and printed in Great Britain by
William Collins Sons & Co. Ltd, Glasgow

Contents

Preface

In this essay I have attempted to examine Mao's thought against the backcloth of the old China which he helped to destroy, as well as from a comparative religious perspective. Although Mao is anti-religious he is evangelical in the true sense; a practical revolutionary. I have referred to certain of Mao's key works which, for various reasons of exposition, I have not taken chronologically. Had I done so, the 1927 *Report of an Investigation of the Peasant Movement in Hunan* would have been the natural starting point, but I have begun rather more metaphysically with his two larger theoretical essays, *On Practice* and *On Contradiction*, both of which date from 1937. Other key essays are *On New Democracy* (1940) and *On the Correct Handling of Contradictions among the People* (1957). The main span is thus thirty years. There is also a short treatment of Mao's poetry.

On the whole I have avoided dealing with other Chinese writers closely associated with Mao, such as Liu Shao-chi, Chou En-lai and Lin Piao. Doubtless, Mao himself would be embarrassed by such writings as *The International Significance of Comrade Mao Tse-Tung's Theory of People's War* by Lin Piao (1965). Naturally, I have made reference to the attitudes of others in the formation of the Mao cult, since this relates directly to the success of Mao's thinking in the remaking of China. Where Mao's writings have been revised – as in the officially published *Selected Works of Mao Tse-Tung* – I have not on the whole taken account of the revisions, since in effect they only reflect the interplay between his thoughts and their success, and, as I argue, part of their meaning, though not exactly their truth, lies in their success.

The roots of this book lie deep in my past. When I went into the army in 1945 I was fortunate enough to go to the Services Unit of Language Training, and in due course the School of Oriental and African Studies for training in the Chinese language. I owe much of my early knowledge of the Chinese world and of Mao to Dr K. Whittaker. In those days I was a kind of Marxist, but she correctly predicted that my sense of humour would ruin my ideological conformity. The more immediate source of this book was an argument with Bryan Magee, who was at that time writing his *Popper*. I was arguing that social democracy had no chance in China because China's problems were special to China. He said that if I felt so strongly about Mao and Mao's role for China, I should write a *Mao*. I am also grateful to Mrs Brenda Almond who has helped with the preparation of the manuscript for the press.

1 Mao and the condition of China

To understand the success of Mao's thought it is essential to measure it against the upheavals which the Chinese had experienced since the beginning of the nineteenth century. No account of Maoism is possible without an evaluation of the events of this period, which led to the need for a recreation of China.

At the time of the Industrial Revolution, the advent of Western sea powers who were primarily concerned with commercial expansion was a shattering experience for the Chinese. Of course China had been used to traders, such as the Arabs, coming from afar and sometimes settling in cities along the coast, and had herself sent out maritime expeditions and knew that nations of some influence existed beyond the sea. Nevertheless, China was still essentially a central land power: like the Roman Empire, it was the inhabited world and the centre of civilization. Those who impinged upon her from without were on the whole treated as barbarians, and so she retained an effortless sense of cultural superiority. Through Chinese eyes the most alarming thing about the Europeans was that despite their cultural inferiority they displayed a staggering power. Moreover, China was not in the best position to resist the new invaders, being under the rule of the declining Manchu dynasty, which was still regarded as foreign despite its assimilation. Its decline was accelerated by the devastating result of the Opium War. The import of opium into China was conducted by the British in order to foster lucrative trade: this meant that the Manchu dynasty had increasingly to co-operate with the British and other foreigners, and allow itself to be deprived of control of customs, one of the most important functions of government. The proliferation of extra-territorial concessions to the foreigners meant that in the latter part of the nineteenth century it looked as though China was on the brink of being carved up into a series of colonies, much as black Africa was divided by some European powers in a scramble for territory and trade. The early manifestations of Chinese nationalism thus had to come to terms with the threat from outside as well as attempting to recreate the ancient central kingdom, and this, together with the fact that the Manchu dynasty itself was relatively foreign, resulted in a certain ambiguity.

This is clearly seen in the Taiping Rebellion – or perhaps more correctly, Revolution – of 1851. There is little doubt that one of the major causes of the Revolution was the Opium War itself, for this drew attention to the problems of rural China in a period of increasing population and dislocation; yet the Taipings turned upon the Manchus more than upon the British and other foreigners. The relationship with the foreign powers was at first relatively amicable, for the new ideology fashioned by the leaders of the Taipings, and notably by Hung Hsiu-ch'üan, owed much to the West, and to Christianity in particular. When two different cultures are in collision, the way towards recreation of the weaker society is often by borrowing some of the elements of the ideology of the stronger. This can be clearly seen in many of the new religious movements in Africa, which are attempts to recreate certain traditional values while at the same time adapting to the new situation. The fact that Hung Hsiu-ch'üan interpreted his dramatic conversion experience in terms of Christianity, partly as a result of his contact with a protestant Christian mission in Canton, was an important factor in his teaching. He argued for collectivism in property, for a radical land reform programme, for equality for women, and for certain moral reforms such as the giving up of tobacco and opium. In addition, the Taipings wanted calendar reform and reform of the literary language to bring it closer to the spoken language. Some of these reforms were put into practice when the Taipings succeeded in dominating a large area of central China – which included the southern capital of Nanking – and in terms of the China of 1851 they were indeed radical. It is self-evident that they anticipated the mood of Mao and his followers at a much later date. Another feature of the Taiping ideology was its vigorous suppression of indigenous religions in the name of a sort of Christianity; images were destroyed and Taoist and Buddhist temples were often wrecked – even the Confucian ancestor-cult was assaulted. Many of the Taipings' ideals persisted long after 1864 when the movement was finally suppressed by the Manchu dynasty.

Another feature of the Taiping Rebellion is noteworthy since it indicates one of the most important pre-conditions of a successful Chinese Revolution. The core of a revolutionary movement had essentially to be the peasants and the poor – though not necessarily the urban poor, or indeed the proletariat. Of course, in 1851 there was no urban proletariat to speak of in China, and despite increasing industrialization during the succeeding fifty years, it is hardly valid to speak of a strong proletariat in the China which Mao was to transform. The number of peasant rebellions is a peculiar feature of Chinese history. Though partly traceable to the friction generated by the traditional mode of land tenure, causes can also be found in natural calamities such as drought and also in population increase. Generally, peasant rebellions were somewhat mindless, but what is remarkable about both the Taiping Rebellion and the Communist Revolution is that they succeeded in giving an ideology and a direction to the fierce dedication which was so easily aroused in the poorer classes by their miserable living conditions. Land reform was at the heart of both movements – though for the Communists it was only a stepping stone to full collectivisation.

It is ironic to reflect that many missionaries initially regarded the Taiping Rebellion as of great importance to the spread of Christianity in China – yet by the end of the affair most Western Christians who were aware of the course of events considered the Taipings heretical, and no longer to be favoured by Western Christian patronage. Western Christianity obviously could not function in China without being adapted somewhat – and this adaptation necessarily amounted to heresy. Similarly, at a later period Western Marxists, including Russians, became disillusioned by the heretical nature of Mao's teachings, though they were well disposed towards the success of Maoism in China at its inception.

Finally, the fact that the Taipings were concerned first of all with rebellion against the Manchu dynasty meant that the movement gave great impetus to criticism of Chinese society. If China were to be reconstructed, it was only possible through radical change in its fundamental institutions. So, the Taipings paved the way for the more extreme Communist ideology.

However, the Taiping Rebellion ended in failure; a failure which the Communists took care to analyse. There were several causes. First, the Taipings never had enough military strength to control more than a limited area of central and southern China. This was due in part to the fact that in the mid nineteenth century communications were poorly developed; and the chances of a totally successful insurrection were a good deal less than in the conditions prevailing some sixty years later. Also, in Mao the Communists had a leader who was capable of making rational and decisive strategic judgements. The Taipings had little idea of the logistics of war.

Secondly, the Taiping ideology was not sufficiently intellectual. Behind successful war there is successful administration – and this for good or ill requires educated bureaucrats. If bureaucrats are *too* educated they become cut off from the people – if they are too ignorant they are ineffective and confused, and this leads to chaos and injustice. The Taiping ideology was essentially populist and no real counterweight to the depth and gravity of the dying Confucian tradition. Mao's Marxism had the intellectual power and analytic discrimination to serve as an instrument of government, but Mao remained ever conscious of the danger of the Marxist functionaries becoming cut off : Whitehall needed to migrate to the farmlands every so often.

Thirdly, the Taipings' leaders made the fatal error of betraying their own ideals when they reached Nanking. Puritanism and concubines do not blend, nor can the contradiction be kept secret in the long run. Although the leadership of the Communist party have had privileges they have been careful not to let power corrupt. In any case, they had a long training in austerity through the long years of struggle – perhaps the Taipings came to power too quickly. It is ironic that effective Puritanism has come more obviously from the Communist initiative than from the quasi-Christian movement.

Fourthly, the Taipings came into some conflict with foreign powers, and for this they were both morally and ideologically ill-equipped. Whereas they had a pro-foreign ideology, partly because of their commitment to a form of Christianity and partly due to their readiness to sacrifice the principle of the centrality of China, the Communists on the other hand, because of their Marxist grounding, had a ready-made anti-foreign theory.

Fifthly, although the Taipings adapted Christianity to Chinese conditions, the Christian ideology was still too foreign to work effectively. Mao's Marxism, though revolutionary and evangelically dynamic, still had in it some echoes of traditional Chinese and Buddhist thinking: its dialectical aspect echoed the surging interplay of the Yin and the Yang, its theory of contradictions reflected some features of Buddhism, and its social orientation reflected the whole basis of Chinese philosophy, where truth is so often seen to reside in social propriety.

Sixthly, the Taipings were too narrowly religious in their dismissal of the whole intellectual and practical world of science and technology. Despite its tendency to dogmatism, Marxism retains a critical and scientific air. A man can have a Marxist faith while retaining a sense of scientific realism – and Christianity has failed to maintain its plausibility in this respect. Though it can be argued that Marxist dogmatism is in the long run the enemy of creative science, this does not invalidate Marxism's vital role in the Chinese process of recreation.

The lessons of Taiping were well digested by the Chinese Communist Party Leadership.

The next important event was the so-called Reform Movement, which came in the wake of China's defeat by Japan. Japan was by now established as a member of the Western club, a status to be dramatically confirmed by her historic victory over Russia in 1905. To be truly Western you had to conduct a successful aggression against another Western nation in a courageous and technological manner – and Japan could not only build iron-clads but could also sport a very stiff upper lip. It was a severe blow for China that her erstwhile pupil in gentlemanly manners, scholarship and spiritual aestheticism should now turn out to have so successfully switched allegiance. Too many Chinese believed the old adage, 'Chinese learning for the basic principles, Western learning for practical application'; but this failed to recognize that ends and means are not so easily disentangled, and also that it was necessary to bring about much more fundamental reforms before China could be strong enough to resist the encroaching West. Hence the Reform Movement, headed by the ardent K'ang Yu-wei who, for a heady hundred days, got the ear of the Emperor and pushed through a great number of reforming edicts.

The ideology of the Reform Movement was merely a version of the quoted adage – while appreciating the need for radical reform and modernization it still claimed to be traditional. This meant that modern meanings were read into the Confucian classics; like the Arya Samaj in India in the nineteenth century, the Reform Movement in China indulged in that well-known syndrome of ancient cultures which have been overtaken – to say 'Anything you can do we did much earlier.' Balm for souls, perhaps, but not for society.

Nevertheless, the Emperor's edicts were impressive: they demanded the introduction of science and technology into teaching, Western-style higher education, Western army training, a reform of the school system, the abolition of the classical civil service examination, a public budget, new methods in agriculture and so on. Although none of these reforms were actually implemented successfully, they did help to loosen up thinking and so prepare the Chinese mind for the future changes. The official Communist analysis of the movement's failure is that the whole programme was abortive since it tried to impose reform from the top. Yet this very scheme had worked in Japan – why not in China?

Part of the answer lies in the decaying and unstable structure of the top echelons of the Empire. After the brief 'reign' of K'ang Yu-wei, government was taken over by the Empress Dowager, Tzu-hsi, and her associates were both ignorant and isolated. However, the basic stumbling-block was historical. The Japanese, though an island people, were not isolationist in principle, and had a tradition of absorbing other traditions – hence their Buddhism, their Sinification, their modern Westernization. The Chinese mind boggled at the idea of borrowing from barbarians – exhibiting the stupidity natural to traditional experts in a changing world. The Reform Movement did not go far enough: it attempted a compromise which was a contradiction in terms.

The Revolution of 1911 attempted to succeed where the Taipings and the Reform Movement had failed. It was more constructive in having a modern ideology, and it did rely on substantial middle-class support. However, Sun Yat-sen and his associates were unused to power politics. So 1911 gave way to 1912 and the era of the pseudo-Emperor Yuan Shih-k'ai; and a decade later the Kuomintang was open to military takeover, and the rise of Chiang Kai-shek. Sun Yat-sen's ideology was not sufficiently dedicated to land reform – the key to a socially successful revolution. An additional factor was that the 1911 revolution relied to a large extent on outside support – especially from imperial powers. In a word, the Kuomintang Revolution was bourgeois.

Chiang Kai-shek had been trained in Moscow but his ideology was right-wing. He wished to destroy the warlords – being himself, as it were, a super-warlord. The massacre of the workers in Shanghai in 1927 was a cynical destruction of the then Left basis of the revolution. The Kuomintang had decided that the future of China lay in the alliance with capitalism and foreign influence.

Apart from the various events in China's pre-revolutionary history mentioned above, there was also the May 4th movement of 1919. This had a profound effect on Mao, and I will examine its effects more closely in a later chapter. Suffice it to say at the present juncture that the outrage at the Treaty of Versailles, which triggered off the May 4th movement, was itself a horrified recognition of the fact that the Western powers and Japan still looked on China as having semi-colonial status. With the coming period of instability and division, it would be another forty years before China could shake off the stigma of colonialism.

Before leaving the prehistory of the Revolution, it is worth examining briefly ideological and cultural developments. The abolition of the Civil Service Examinations in the early 1900s had a shattering effect on the educational system and was the signal for a profound disillusionment with Confucianism. An increasing proportion of young intellectuals was going abroad for its education, and in any event higher education in China itself was dominated by Western models and ideas. Taoism as a system of beliefs had a hidden revival, in the sense that anarchism had a certain appeal among left-wing groups. Despite signs of vigour in Buddhism, the predominant mood of reformers and revolutionaries was that the old religions made people too passive, and that these beliefs were not really compatible with modern science – which was often very imperfectly understood. There was, then, a great ideological vacuum which the programme of the Kuomintang hoped to fill. Meanwhile, a literary revolution towards a less archaic written style was taking place, and the whole process of language reform was part of the movement to modernize China. In the period after World War I, China was indeed in a state of ferment. It would take over a quarter of a century to resolve the conflicts and to impose on China a new uniformity.

2 Mao – a brief biography

There are of course some excellent biographies of Mao (some of these are mentioned in the bibliography), and my aim in this brief sketch is to set the scene of his intellectual development.

Born in 1893 in the village of Shao Shun in Hunan, Mao was the son of a poor peasant who, however, managed to become relatively well-to-do. Mao's father was mean and severe and there were many clashes between them – Mao displayed an early independence of spirit. His mother was simply an illiterate, kindly, pious Buddhist. Mao had some primary schooling and later gained admission to the school in Ch'angsha, where in 1911 he witnessed the events of the Revolution, and for a few months he served in the Revolutionary Army. His early schooling had introduced him to the classics and as a boy he was an avid reader of Chinese novels, especially such heroic adventures as *The Water Margin*. In Ch'angsha he became acquainted with a whole mass of Western literature, mainly non-fictional works on philosophy, history, politics and economics. He was a voracious reader – a habit which lasted throughout his active life. It was an exciting period of intellectual ferment. Mao was by this time strongly nationalist, and in 1918 he founded the New Citizens Society, a discussion group of young people. He and his friends were also at this time strongly devoted to physical culture : mental and physical culture went together. In that year also he went to Peking, hoping to enrol in the university – instead (for he was penniless) he got a menial job in the university library. However, he was able to pursue his reading, and was also helped and influenced by Li Ta-chao, an early Marxist. From this period on Mao was moving steadily in the direction of Marxism. In 1919 he returned to Ch'angsha and edited a radical weekly for a while. He revisited Peking and next year went to Shanghai, working as a laundryman to make ends meet. More importantly, however, in the summer of 1921 he was one of twelve members at the First Congress of the Chinese Communist Party. Because it was Red policy to work with and within the

Kuomintang, Mao was a delegate to the KMT Congress in 1924, and was elected to the Central Executive, becoming editor of its propaganda publication, *Political Weekly*. Meanwhile he had had a spell as teacher in Ch'angsha and had married his first wife (a childhood marriage arranged by his family had never been consummated, and Mao later repudiated it). His wife was captured in Ch'angsha and beheaded in 1930 – many of Mao's relatives died bloodily, including his son Mao An-ying, in 1950 in Korea.

1924 marked the beginning of a three-year period of intense organizational work, including the setting up of peasant units. His *Report of an Investigation of the Peasant Movement* of 1927 was of considerable importance in his theoretical development. In 1927 Chiang's coup in Shanghai and massacre of many Communists, socialists, workers and peasants, both in the city and in the Hunanese countryside, caused Mao to organize a worker-peasant army and start an uprising in Hunan and Kiangsi. Though this was a failure, and he narrowly escaped death when taken prisoner, he managed to concentrate some forces in the wild and mountainous area of Ching-kangshan in Kiangsi – and there the core of the Soviet base developed. This was the beginning of a series of fierce struggles with the KMT who brought large forces to bear on the Red area. Little documentation has survived from this period, but no doubt Mao was beginning to form his ideas on mobile and guerilla warfare.

In May 1934 Chiang's ring of steel proved too strong and tight and by October the position seemed desperate. The Reds decided to break out to move towards another Soviet area in Kweichow. It was the start of the Long March, in which six and a half thousand miles were covered, landing Mao and a remnant of his forces in Shensi in the north-west. Most important, it was at a conference at Tsunyi during the Long March that Mao finally gained leadership and control of the CCP. It was here too that the Party adopted the slogan, 'Go North to fight the Japanese'.

The strategy of a united front with the KMT was formed with some hesitation in the North-West. This was the prelude to eight years of war against the Japanese: it was also a fruitful period for Mao intellectually and some of his major writings date from the Yenan days. There he met and married in 1939 his second wife, Chiang Ch'ing. She exerted a major influence in shaping his interest in the arts.

After the Japanese surrender various unsuccessful attempts were made to prevent the civil war breaking out again. In 1949 Mao was able to stand before a huge crowd in Peking to proclaim the foundation of the People's Republic. The major internal events thereafter were the period of the Hundred Flowers (1956), the Great Leap Forward (1958), and the Cultural Revolution (1967). The last was over by 1970, and an era of new politics and détente followed this. Mao's leadership has been threatened on two or three occasions in this post-liberation era, but he has established himself as an indispensable *éminence grise*.

This then, in brief, was the life framework of Mao's ideas.

3 Mao on practice

Mao's two major theoretical works dating from the pre-War period are *On Practice* and *On Contradiction*. They both belong to 1937, though the latter was not published until 1952. There is no reason, however, to suspect that it was backdated to show Mao's relatively early role as a developer of the Marxist-Leninist tradition. What is interesting is the audience: for it was necessarily in the years between 1937 and 1952 an inner party document. In brief, it was practical theorizing. This is in accord with Mao's whole message in *On Practice*. Both documents were delivered as lectures in the so-called Anti-Japanese Military and Political College in Yenan. This is an indication of their context – a context in which the Communist Party was turning to co-operation with Chiang Kai-shek in the struggle against the Japanese. It was a difficult time for the party and the drive which kept the movement going was, of course, Marxism-Leninism. Mao was alive to the danger that this 'red bible' could be too rigidly adhered to, and one of his main aims was to make thinking amongst the CCP leaders and workers more flexible.

In *On Practice* Mao begins by saying that before Marx the theory of knowledge was divorced from social conditions; therefore the way in which knowledge depends upon social practice, production and the class struggle was obscured. It is interesting to note that here Mao implicitly subscribes to a 'one tradition' view of the history of philosophy – almost as though the Chinese tradition of philosophical thinking never really existed. However, in *On Contradiction* Mao does make a brief reference to dialectical thinking in ancient China, but characterizes it as having 'a somewhat spontaneous and naïve character'. He was probably referring to the old Chinese notion of the interplay between the Yin and the Yang; that is, between the male and female principles underlying cosmic and earthly changes. But in viewing Mao's attitude to the philosophical and religious past, we must remember some important parts of his own life. He is said to have hated Confucius since childhood (or so he told Edgar Snow), and Confucianism with all its accretions was still, despite the abolition of the classical civil service examinations in the early part of the century, ideologically entangled with the feudalism in the rural world in which Mao was born and worked. Precisely because so much of Chinese philosophy was socially oriented, it could not be a strong force in a period when the whole fabric of society was breaking down. Mao recognized the need for a new social ideology and his discovery of Marxism was enthusiastic.

In *On Practice* Mao goes on to give a fairly straightforward account of the development of knowledge from a Marxist point of view. Only with the emergence of the proletariat with the growth of large-scale industry was man able to acquire a comprehensive understanding of the way society changes, and to turn this knowledge into a science, namely the science of Marxism. One aspect of the 'practical' emphasis of Marxism is that only by social practice is knowledge acquired – and here Mao is referring to material production, class struggle and scientific experiment.

How does Mao attempt to justify this theory of knowledge? Part of the answer is in his idea of the nature of the things of which we aim to acquire knowledge. Leaving aside the physical world for the moment, and looking to the world of man in society, Mao subscribes to the doctrine that men are importantly constituted by their relationships. These relationships are shifting owing to the process of historical change, and therefore it is impossible to arrive at a static essence of society. For this reason all knowledge of man in society is itself dated – for it is only knowledge of people living at a certain date, in certain social conditions. Further knowledge arises through experimenting, as it were, with the relationships. So it is by action that social knowledge is acquired. I shall call this 'the social interference theory of knowledge' and shall in due course try to make an evaluation of it.

As for the world of physical nature, Mao holds that here too knowledge comes from interference. He looks upon experimentation as essentially interference with matter – thus, if you want to know the inner nature of an atom you must change the atom's structure by bombarding it with particles.

Mao goes on to relate this to the notion that knowledge involves direct experience, which he rather loosely describes as perception – and all knowledge is based either on personal or related experience. So the development of knowledge is necessarily a collective enterprise. Mao stresses that scientific knowledge requires complete honesty and modesty. 'How can you catch tiger cubs without going into the tiger's lair?' he asks, quoting an old Chinese proverb. So far, then, Mao's rather simply stated theory implies that knowledge is the result of activity and experience in a shared collective enterprise. It is also conditioned by its historical context.

Mao adds to this a dialectical account of the relationship between experience and theory (between, as he puts it, perceptual and conceptual knowledge). For him perceptions and impressions do not by themselves give any deep understanding, but are simply the start of a road that leads to the ultimate goal, of uncovering the essential nature of reality. By reflecting on impressions one comes to see the internal relationship of things and events. This in turn leads to the dialectical-materialist understanding of reality.

In a number of passages Mao suggests that the appearances of things are fragmentary and indeed misleading, so that a man without the backing of theory is in a kind of daze of sense-data. Thus Mao would argue that empiricism is an absurd account of the world. Yet repeated experiences give rise to concepts, as we classify them together; so it is a creative daze which gradually can drive us to a deeper theoretical grasp of the nature of the world.

Mao gives some straightforwardly political examples of knowledge as he understands it. Thus he remarks that the proletariat in the early stages of capitalism – the era of machine-smashing and sporadic rioting – had only perceptual cognition; for it only noticed some of the outer aspects and relations of the phenomena of capitalism. It is clear here how loosely he is using the term 'perception', for a certain amount of theory-laden belief animated the Luddites. He goes on to explain that it was only with the development of a comprehensive way of understanding capitalism, in the theories of Marx and Engels, that the proletariat reached the stage of rational knowledge. These theories themselves arose in part from the conscious and organized struggles of the working class. In its perception of the nature of capitalism the proletariat also became self-aware – a 'class for itself'. Thus a change in perception is brought about by the acquisition of rational knowledge – a dialectical interplay between the two levels.

Mao goes on to illustrate further with some Chinese examples. He considers that the Taipings, the Boxers and others, reacting rather indiscriminately to foreign powers, represented a perception of imperialism. It was only at a later time that rational knowledge replaced this. Interestingly, he dates this knowledge from about the May 4th Movement of 1919. The truth perceived thereafter was that imperialism had allied itself to the comprador and feudal classes in China in order to exploit the masses of the Chinese people. The dating is interesting for 1919 antedates the founding of the Chinese Communist Party by two years. Mao was much influenced and impressed by the May 4th Movement for its exposition of the connection between feudalism and imperialism. This meant that it was a great advance on the Revolution of 1911. One reason why the latter could not solve China's problems was that it was aimed at the feudal structure (of which the Emperor was the key symbol) but not at imperialism, whereas it was only by attacking both that China could be liberated. From this perspective Mao blended Chinese nationalism with social reformism. They were two sides of one coin. He wrote:

The May 4th Movement possessed this quality because capitalism had developed a step further in China and because new hopes had arisen for the liberation of the Chinese nation as China's revolutionary intellectuals saw the collapse of three great imperialist powers, Russia, Germany and Austria-Hungary, and the weakening of two others, Britain and France, while the Russian proletariat had established a socialist state and the German, Hungarian and Italian proletariat had risen in revolution . . . In the beginning the May 4th Movement was the revolutionary movement of a united front of three sections of people – Communist intellectuals, revolutionary petty-bourgeois intellectuals and bourgeois intellectuals.

But he goes on to say that with June 3rd and the strike in Shanghai the Movement became a nationwide revolutionary movement:

The cultural revolution ushered in by the May 4th Movement was uncompromising in its opposition to feudal culture;

there had never been such a great and thoroughgoing cultural revolution since the dawn of Chinese history.

We cannot of course fail to reflect that he was to try to match 1919 in 1967, with the great proletarian cultural revolution.

To return to Mao's account of knowledge – here he very explicitly draws out the social basis of theory. It is by action and in this case collective action that the real nature of China's predicament became known.

But Mao considers that the transition from perceptual to theoretical knowledge is still only a beginning, for although it is true that revolution requires theory, and is otherwise just a blind and fragmentary struggle, the theory itself needs application. Mao continually stresses the need to be adaptable in the way Marxism-Leninism is applied to concrete conditions. At the time he was writing it was, as we have seen, important to wean many away from a Red fundamentalism. In the course of concrete application it may be necessary to revise and modify one's views and actions. One should always test theory against objective reality. But how is this done?

Again, by social practice. In the essay Mao draws on his experience of warfare. The theoretical part of Marxism-Leninism is like a military manual; it is only any good if it actually works, and you find that out by trying out the lessons of the handbook in actual combat. Mao goes on to remark that revolutionary leaders must always be flexible and capable of learning lessons from the historical process as that develops.

Towards the conclusion of his essay Mao states that the present moment in human history is unprecedented: 'the moment for completely banishing darkness from the world and from China and for changing the world into a world of light such as never previously existed.'

So much then for Mao's essay *On Practice*. We shall see later how it connects up with his doctrine of contradiction. Meanwhile let us evaluate it.

First, we should repeat that part of Mao's aim was to undermine 'Red fundamentalism', as I have called it. The danger of trying to assimilate a system of foreign ideas is that they are adhered to much too blindly – it can become mechanical materialism, as Mao dubs it. From this perspective *On Practice* is a major theoretical move to loosen up Marxism so that it could be applied flexibly to the Chinese scene. The document is therefore complementary to the more practically oriented *Report on an Investigation of the Peasant Movement in Hunan*.

Secondly, its general philosophy is not worked out in any fine detail. Some of its theories are open to criticism. For instance, though Mao is no doubt correct to reject empiricism as he understands it, he is too experimentalist in his account of the generation of theories. Some quite highly developed sciences, such as astronomy, have depended more on observation than experiment. It is difficult to see in what sense the moon is changed or interfered with when it is being observed through a telescope. Again, Mao has little to say about the role of conceptual revolutions in the progress of human knowledge and does not even mention non-experimental areas of knowledge, such as mathematics.

However, it could be that what I have called the social interference theory of knowledge may be applied correctly to social areas of experience, even if it does not have any close analogy to what happens in the physical sciences. But in what sense could Mao be correct in his example of the May 4th Movement? First of all it is important to notice the valuational element in the supposed knowledge, for the discernment of a close alliance between imperialism and feudalism in the exploitation of the masses of China is obviously intended to be the discernment also of the forces against which the Chinese people should struggle. Imperialism is not just a neutral phenomenon. Now where valuation enters in, it could be argued that knowledge does imply direct experience and action, for unless you have climbed a mountain you do not know how tiring and exhilarating it is (tiring is otherwise bad, and exhilaration – other things being equal – good). That Monte Crocione is 5000 feet above sea level is to be *known*. That it is nice to climb is an evaluative opinion.

Large issues can turn upon the separation of fact from value (a theoretical position put more linguistically, but very forcibly, in much recent analytic philosophy). For, if the split is enforced, it leaves a breathing-space for pure scholarship and pure science. Whatever the values present in society they are, on the fact-value dichotomy theory, independent of the truth and scientific and scholarly conclusions. The dichotomy thus favours the independence of science and in institutional terms favours the autonomy of institutions of learning, such as universities. Of course there could be arguments for this even if the dichotomy theory were abandoned, but it surely makes the autonomy easier. An anti-Japanese university, as at Yenan, would seem to be a contradiction, unless perhaps the anti-Japanese was merely contingent, like Duke University in America being founded by someone called Duke.

However, the dichotomy theory is not quite true. I think we need a rather sophisticated way of dealing with the variety of relations between facts and values, for the degree of implication between factual and valuational utterances is variable, from entailment through suggestion to independence. For example, in order to understand the concept *compassion* you have to have not only the relevant attitude but also (other things being equal) to treat it as a good attitude. To put it crudely, the statement 'Compassion is a good attitude' is necessarily true. Towards the other end of the scale, you can understand cricket but disagree as to its worth. Some people see glory in cricket and some do not: 'Cricket is a good game' is alas *not* necessarily true. Still, that men find glory in it is merely a point in its favour. To take a more extreme illustration, whether the greenness of grass is a good thing or not is obscure – it is simply a fact of life. You can protest that green is a symbol of fertility, but it is a *symbol* only. Consider this statement – 'There are some grains of sand in the bottom of the nearest coalmine' – it is hard to know what valuational utterance *that* implies.

To all of this it may be replied that contexts may supply implications. This I accept; and there is always something artificial in citing bald statements as examples. Nevertheless, I think it is reasonable to hold to a sliding scale to modify the dichotomy.

Mao's doctrine could have some somewhat limited application across the spectrum of types of knowledge in view of this sliding scale, for it may be that social action against imperialism and feudalism in the May 4th Movement and its aftermath was a way of acquiring attitudes through practical and hostile action. These attitudes may be at least heavily implied by the concepts of imperialism and feudalism given that one is Chinese and not being either imperialist or feudal.

There is also another side of the coin, since the discernment of the 'true nature' of the forces controlling and interfering with China was also a discernment of one's own nature. The

Chinese intellectuals and proletariat involved in the Movement saw their own nature through their actions. If a man woos a woman he sees his own nature as a lover and as a male practically and, as we say, existentially, in a manner no amount of non-wooing can achieve.

This then is the degree of truth in Mao's doctrine. For the rest, there have been dangers, for the doctrine can be a licence for foreclosing upon pure science – the imaginative and speculative element in human researches and thoughts. It is perhaps no coincidence that the Cultural Revolution exerted some of its most powerful impact in the world of higher education. It is perhaps also no coincidence that among the Hundred Flowers were a thousand weeds – weeds from Mao's point of view.

How far is *On Practice* in accord with Marxism-Leninism? Does it mean a departure? Is it novel? I do not myself see that the doctrines of *On Practice* can be shown to be incompatible with the tradition out of which they came, though it is true that the emphasis is more practical. Mao was a man of action; he urged people not to read too much, not even *too* much of Marx – a nice irony, but also one which hints at a lack of strong devotion to detailed data for theory. So although *On Practice* is Marxist, it is not quite in the spirit of Marx.

There are in *On Practice* hints of a certain Chineseness, though this comes out much more clearly in *On Contradiction* – to be discussed later. But it is worth remarking that before 1937 Mao had read very little Communist literature. Very few of the Marxist classics were translated until the late 1930s – indeed from Mao's point of view not until the Yenan period, so perhaps one should look on *On Practice* and *On Contradiction* as reactions to a new view of Marxism as mediated by the new translations. Also they are essays aimed at establishing Mao's position as an ideologue. From Lenin onwards political leaders needed also to be theoretical leaders. This got Stalin, who was no intellectual, into a lot of trouble. But Mao *was* an intellectual in his own fashion and this made his ideological leadership very natural.

But it would be wrong to look at his writing of these two essays as a matter of establishing a certain prestige. It is quite sincere of him to reckon that theory is necessary to practice – to maintain that the revolution needed a theory to guide it. The two essays were meant to be part of that guidance, at a crucial time when the Communists were becoming involved in the fight against Japan – the Japan which had adapted, after all, the role of a colonialist power.

In brief, *On Practice* is seminal, but its teachings are open to question. They are important, if somewhat naïve, but constitute only the prelude to *On Contradiction*, Mao's more vital theoretical work.

4 Mao on contradiction

In *On Contradiction*, more clearly than anywhere else, Mao encapsulates his total view of life. That view helps to explain much that came later – for example, the Great Leap Forward and the Cultural Revolution, phenomena that have puzzled many commentators because the wrong criteria were used to evaluate them. Neither of these episodes seemed successful – were they not both ultimately called off? Did they not in their different ways produce a fair amount of chaos? The many small steel-making outfits in rural China were scarcely efficient. The Great Leap caused extensive economic dislocation, and how much more disruptive was the Cultural Revolution? But two facets of Mao's thinking must be kept in mind. First, there is his emphasis on continuing struggle – an emphasis which encourages a periodic shake-up, even at the expense of some normal economic and political aims. Secondly, Mao emphasizes the mental or spiritual aspect of revolutionary development. Thus both the Great Leap and the Cultural Revolution are justified by their mental and spiritual effect: the Great Leap gave many peasants a more technological outlook, and helped to break down the barrier between town worker and rural worker; the Cultural Revolution reshaped people's attitudes towards criticism both in the Party and in education. Both these somewhat cataclysmic events flow directly from Mao's thinking as expressed in his 1937 essay, *On Contradiction*. We shall also see that it is in this essay above all that Mao reflects the influence of earlier Chinese thought: there is in it an intuitive adaptation to a Chinese style of elements drawn from the Marxist tradition.

Mao begins his essay with a quotation from Lenin. Incidentally, he tends to stress the contribution of Lenin, and this is part of his theory of the correlation between historical changes and the development of Marxist doctrine. Thus Lenin's importance lies in his capacity to analyse the phenomenon of imperialism, living as he did during its apogee. So Mao himself, living in different conditions and in another epoch, can develop the doctrine further. He praises Stalin for remarking that now communist revolution can turn its attention to the East, but obviously the conditions in the East differ from those in Europe and Russia – so once again we see the need for an extra phase of Marxism. Later the doctrinal tradition was thus referred to as Marxist-Leninist-Mao Tse-tung thought.

To return to the quotation from Lenin: 'Dialectics in the proper sense is the study of contradiction *in the very essence of* objects.' This is very much Mao's slogan. In *On Practice* he referred to perceptions as liable to give a superficial knowledge unless one penetrates deeper to the true nature of things. This true nature is to be found in the operation of contradictions. Beneath the shifting haze of sense-data these are the deep, resounding tensions. The shifting haze tells you something – for one thing, its *shifting* is a sign that everything is in motion, and contradiction is as it were the fuel that keeps everything in motion. Put more prosaically, 'This dialectical world outlook teaches us primarily how to observe and analyse the movement of opposites in different things.' And, as in *On Practice*, the theory has a practical outcome since it enables us to resolve contradictions on the basis of the analysis.

This point is, of course, important. It might be argued that if contradictions are universal and all-pervasive it is rather foolish to attempt to resolve them. It will only mean that new contradictions arise. But there is implicit in Mao's (and Marxist) thinking the recognition that the historical dialectic is progressive. This is not to deny that disasters or setbacks can occur. In that respect progress is not inevitable, but the resolution of contradictions does bring progress, and the general drift of the dialectical process is progressive. However, disasters can occur; there is a constant Banquo at Mao's feast – the spectre of backsliding, the possibility that ultimately the revolution and writings and killings in the end prove to have been the harbingers of a mere alternative bureaucracy. In 1937 Mao was not yet so worried by that ghost – Banquos haunt those who are kings, and Mao was not yet king. What he certainly *was* worried about was dogmatism, the waving of the Red Bible. So he slides neatly into his argument in *On Contradiction* by remarking that

I shall deal first with the universality of contradiction and then proceed to the particularity of contradiction. The reason is that the universality of contradiction can be explained more briefly . . . whereas the particularity of contradiction is still not clearly understood by many comrades, and especially by the dogmatists.

Mao's claim to be an original thinker in the Marxist tradition lies in this emphasis upon the particularity of contradiction.

In a nice paradox Mao remarks that it is precisely in the particularity of contradiction that the universality of contradiction resides. In other words we can know in advance that in some process there is a contradiction (or a set of them), but we do not thereby know its actual nature, for that depends upon the particular aspects of the process which are in contradiction. Needless to say, Mao uses the term 'contradiction' in a wide sense, sometimes to include logical contradictions (as when he talks about competing theories put forward within the Party), sometimes contraries (victory and defeat in battle, for example), sometimes simply opposing forces within a process. This plurality of the concept is another reason always for examining the particular.

In turning to his discussion of the particular Mao follows Lenin fairly closely in his materialism. For Mao there is nothing at all in the world except matter in motion. Each form of motion contains its own special contradiction, and this constitutes its essence – this is the reason for the multiplicity of things in the world – its great variety (what older writers called the 10,000 things). He also makes a plea not just for studying the essence of each form of matter and motion, but also for seeing it in its process of development. Every genuine development involves a change of quality. This has a practical consequence, for it means that where A develops into B the method used for resolving the contradiction in B must now be different from the method used in relation to A. This is good common sense; and Mao illustrates it with political examples. The contradiction between proletariat and bourgeoisie is resolved by socialist revolution; between the masses and feudalism by democratic revolution (this is, of course, the phrase for the first main phase of revolution in China – we shall be returning to this in contemplating the essay *On New Democracy*) and so on. What is interesting is that as early as 1937 Mao anticipated the continuance of struggle within the Communist Party : he writes that the contradiction within the Party has to be resolved by criticism. He was later, in his *On the*

Correct Handling of Contradictions among the People of 1957, to elaborate this whole part of his doctrine.

The principle that one should use different methods to resolve different contradictions is another theoretical licence to develop strategy differently in China from the way it had been developed in Russia – a point overlooked by the dogmatists, says Mao. This was always implicit in Mao's pragmatism at the outset of his revolutionary career, in his *Peasant Movement Report*.

In the next section of the essay Mao goes on to distinguish between the principal contradiction in a complex whole and the lesser ones, and to distinguish the principal aspect of a contradiction from the other. The latter point has a vital application. Thus he writes:

> When the superstructure (politics, culture, etc.) obstructs the development of the economic base, political and cultural changes become principal and decisive. Are we going against materialism when we say this? The reason is that while we recognize that in the general development of history the material determines the mental and social being social consciousness, we also – and indeed must – recognize the reaction of the mental on material things, of social consciousness on social being and of the superstructure of the economic base. This does not go beyond materialism; on the contrary, it avoids mechanical materialism . . .

Here is the basis of Mao's developing voluntarism.

The ceaseless surge of the dialectic is, for Mao, everywhere apparent, and its rhythms bring about the unity of opposites and then new oppositions. Mao elaborates on the way opposites pass into one another. Thus to set up the dictatorship of the proletariat is to prepare the conditions for abolishing it, for the state apparatus is due eventually to wither away. So, likewise, to establish and build the Communist Party is to prepare the way for the elimination of it and all other political parties.

There is no doubt that these anarchistic dreams were taken quite seriously by Mao – always concerned with modes of devolution. The communes of the Great Leap period were a move in the direction of anarchism, likewise the use of the Red Guards to criticize the Party was a reminder of the possibility of its ultimate demise. However, these dreams were counterbalanced by a strong sense of the great length of time needed to achieve the full success of the revolution. Mao is in part here influenced by his vision of perpetual struggle, and in no doubt as regards the problems created by both the Great Leap and the Cultural Revolution. Also, it must seem strange that someone so dedicated and long suffering as Lin Piao, who had struggled by his side in the amazing epic in which the Communists had finally won power in all China, should betray him. Close at hand there is plenty of evidence to temper optimism about changing human, and Chinese, nature. So the struggle goes on. But we should not lose sight of the seriousness with which Mao appears to have taken the doctrine of the withering away of the state.

The main point Mao wishes to make in regard to the identity of opposites is that the achievement of this is conditional and ultimately less important than the struggle of opposites, which is absolute. His reasoning on this point is as follows. There are two types of motion, one being relative rest and the other conspicuous change. In the first case a being is kept in a state of unity by the tensions within it as between the opposites struggling together – it is rather like two cards leaning against each other. However, the equilibrium will in due course be disturbed, and then we have a qualitative – i.e. a conspicuous – change. The original unity is broken up. Now since it is only in certain conditions that the unity is maintained, this unity is conditional and relative; but since struggle occurs both in the unity and in the conspicuous change, it is absolute. This is a moving picture of the world, virtually the opposite of Plato : not for Mao a picture of true reality as static and eternal.

Mao goes on to qualify what he says about struggle, and in the next section of the essay he anticipates some questions he was later to deal with in *On the Correct Handling of Contradictions among the People*. Indeed, the relation between the two works is one reason for the special interest taken in *On Contradiction* in the period after 1957. Mao distinguishes between antagonistic and non-antagonistic contradictions. In effect this is a distinction between relatively violent and relatively non-violent tensions between classes, factions, town and countryside, and so on.

These, then, are the main ideas in *On Contradiction*. It is clear that Mao owes much to Lenin; but the overwhelming emphasis in Mao's work is on the increasing tension and flux

M   B in the world and in history, and his ideas have an interesting analogy to some earlier strands in eastern thought.

For example, the doctrine of the Void in Chinese Mahayana Buddhism implied that contradiction lies at the heart of all phenomena, and there are echoes of Mao in Neo-Confucianism. I shall reserve discussion of such analogies until a later chapter where I shall attempt to evaluate the 'Chineseness' of Mao.

It can scarcely be felt that much in the way of tight argument enters into *On Contradiction*; in the main it is a somewhat dogmatic presentation of a picture of the world. What are the features which made this picture sufficiently attractive to act as the fuel for the Chinese revolutionary movement?

First, materialism could come to terms with the scientific outlook which was one of the West's contributions to the turmoil of the Chinese spirit. In particular the materialism by being dynamic and by reducing everything to motion could plausibly be held to be a general framework in which physics could be understood. Naturally this effect is achieved by the very imprecision of such ideas as motion in Mao's exposition.

Secondly, the idea that the superstructure and cultural values could be the determining factor at a certain stage of history gave Maoism the advantages of idealism without the disadvantages. It could retain the practical emphasis of dialectical materialism but at the same time appeal to the fact that faith does move mountains. Even more than most Marxists, Mao stresses the importance of correct attitudes; but beyond that he is candid about their strong causative role in the revolutionary process. One reason for this was that China's crisis was in large measure spiritual : it was not like the problems in Europe where to a great extent the tensions caused by the Industrial Revolution were not to do with loss of cultural nerve – on the contrary, the cultures of Europe, and even the culture of Russia, marginal as always to the European phenomenon, were relatively self-confident. All this could not be said of China, for reasons which we have pointed to earlier. So Mao's voluntarism had an appeal for those wishing to recreate the Chinese essence, and this voluntarism has its ideological justification in *On Contradiction*.

Thirdly, the ideology of perpetual struggle suited a period when the light at the end of the tunnel was hardly visible. It is no doubt one reason for Mao's own persistent and strong determination not to compromise except for an intermediate and theoretically justifiable end, and in this he could as it were console himself with the thought of the long road. The Long March is part of that long road, stretching onwards into the world's history.

Fourthly, the picture of the world in flux appeals to a sense of impermanence that is found in Chinese culture both from Taoist and from (obviously) Buddhist sources. However, the flux is not now conceived as a ground for rising beyond it to the emptiness of the eternal; rather it is looked on in an activist way as a stream to be navigated. By navigating the flux a new heaven will be created, hopefully – but not a nirvana.

Fifthly, incipiently in *On Contradiction* there is a kind of anarchism which could appeal to revolutionaries bent on destroying a feudal China, but whose conception of democracy was scarcely well developed, partly because of Marxist theory – for democratic institutions as understood in the West were categorized by Mao as bourgeois and only just contrasted to bourgeois fascism (though there is no great evidence that Mao knew a vast amount about European history; just as the Westerners who opposed Mao knew little of Chinese history).

Sixthly, there is in *On Contradiction* a pedagogical method, crude but no doubt effective, and also perhaps deriving from Mao's experience as a teacher. This method relates to the doctrine of the questions of the principal contradiction and of the aspect which is more important in the process in question. Mao urges people to analyse, and it is characteristic that in his writings he not only urges analysis but also shows a rough and ready method of doing it. This is not to be despised because it is not highly sophisticated – for the basis of action cannot easily be a learned culture. Indeed part of Mao's secret has been his discriminating crudity.

The two works we have been considering date from 1937. It is now useful to go back to Mao's report of ten years earlier. This is not very theoretical, but it had a great importance in shaping the direction of the Chinese revolution. Then we can proceed to *On the Correct Handling of Contradictions among the People*, which quite closely relates to *On Contradiction*.

5 Mao on the Hunanese peasants

When Mao went down to Hunan to investigate the peasant movement he was already sympathetic to what was emerging as a new form of rural rebellion. Already in March 1926 he had written his essay *An Analysis of the Classes in Chinese Society* which pointed to the later strategies of the Chinese Communist Party. Briefly, his analysis was as follows.

Given that the problems of China were related both to feudalism and imperialism, one should look at the role of classes connected with these phenomena. In rural China the old structure remained and this depended upon the landlord system. (It is true that in China there was not the system of *latifundia* which has characterized parts of Europe – the landlords were generally local gentry, and culturally related to the official class which kept the system going.) So one class which needed to be singled out as an enemy is the landlord class, and this was linked with the comprador class. Since capitalism had entered China entangled with imperialism, part of the bourgeoisie in effect worked for imperialist interests – and this is what Mao refers to as the comprador class. Originally the term meant the Chinese manager of a European-owned factory or business, but Mao extended its meaning to cover all those whose interests were closely integrated with imperialist capitalism. Since, in Mao's view, China's feudal structure also subserved imperialist interests, the landlords and the comprador class were the prime targets of revolutionary activity.

But Mao distinguished the compradors from the middle bourgeoisie, most of whom constituted what was called the 'national bourgeoisie'. These men had business interests which in part conflicted with imperialism, and also they often displayed patriotism and some support for revolutionary activities insofar as these were anti-foreign. However, Mao did not consider them to be sufficiently strong to be the basis of a bourgeois democratic regime. This was partly because the foundation of the Soviet state and other events showed the strength of the International, injecting a new element into the

flow of historical events; and partly because the Chinese
bourgeoisie was split (as also was the gentry). So the conditions
in China were not classical. There was no real question in
Mao's mind at this stage of going through the phase of
bourgeois democracy before that of a socialist revolution.
Though it would be a long struggle the classic sequence would
be shortcircuited. The moral to be drawn from this analysis
was that co-operation with the national bourgeoisie in the
struggle against foreign domination could be fruitful. This,
however, was not necessarily to mean co-operation with the
Kuomintang – even in 1926 the tensions which were to erupt
in 1927 were beginning to be felt.

The next class is the petty bourgeoisie, consisting of the
middle peasants, i.e. those who owned land and had enough
to make a reasonable livelihood, together with craftsmen,
lower level intellectuals such as teachers and minor officials,
students and small traders. There are according to Mao three
varieties of petty bourgeoisie. There are those who have some
surplus and want to get rich – they are on the edge of the
middle bourgeoisie and look up to them. Then there are those
who want to get rich but are simply stuck in the system.
Finally there are those whose standard of living is actually
falling – they become bitter against foreigners, warlords and
so on, and are quite important from a revolutionary point of
view.

The next class – and one that was to form the major part of
Mao's power base – was what he called the semi-proletariat.
Some of these were poor peasants who owned some land but
had to rent more to make ends meet. Also the poor peasants
who do not own land and have to give up half or more of the
crop as rent. Some of these have so little reserves (in the shape
of tools, etc.) that they have to sell their labour very cheaply
and often need to eke out a living by begging. They are
typically burdened by debt. These two groups, the semi-owners
and the poor peasants, represent the overwhelming mass of
the rural population. As a separate group there are the small
craftsmen, shop workers, pedlars, and so on.

Then there is the industrial proletariat proper, which Mao
estimated in 1926 as numbering about two million. In addition
to industrial workers, there are coolies and rural labourers.
All these have nothing to their name but their hands and backs.
Mao also mentions the lumpen-proletariat of dispossessed

peasants, out-of-work craftsmen and so on. They often turn to banditry and piracy and, Mao avers, are brave fighters and could be useful to the revolution, even if they are apt to be destructive. In fact, quite a number were to take part in the fighting at Chingkangshan, the first Red base in South China, and they had been formerly a relatively powerful element in the Taiping Revolution. In the original version of this early essay, Mao's description of bandits was somewhat romantic, influenced no doubt by his childhood reading. There are also important references to the various secret societies, which were vehicles for organizing extra-societal groups.

Such then is Mao's survey of classes. He is already moving to his main position as expressed in the *Peasant Movement* Report. He concludes:

> To sum up, it can be seen that our enemies are all those in league with imperialism – the warlords, the bureaucrats, the comprador class, the big landlord class and the reactionary section of the intelligentsia attached to them. The leading force in our revolution is the industrial proletariat. Our closest friends are the entire semi-proletariat and petty bourgeoisie. As for the vacillating middle bourgeoisie, their right-wing may become our enemy and their left-wing may become our friend . . .

Such, then, was Mao's position in 1926. The basic analysis of classes has remained with him through his career. Note how in the end he is *mainly* interested in combating imperialism. Marxism was unconsciously a means of restoring China's substance.

Peasant rebellion had been erupting in Hunan and elsewhere. It was to some extent being directed by the Communists and other workers, and occurred in the wake of the drive by the Northern Expeditionary Army of the Kuomintang. Unlike most previous peasant uprisings it was well organized, and Mao refers to it not unreasonably as 'a great revolution in the countryside, a revolution without parallel in history'. He was quite clear that doctrinaire concentration on the industrial revolution and too much co-operation with the moderates of the Kuomintang would be fatal. Events in Shanghai were to prove him right. What is indisputable is that the peasant movement made a powerful impact on him. He was also beginning to think of weaving into it a military dimension, and it was therefore at this period that he began to formulate the doctrine of revolution by insurrection and military enclave – in other words, to conform to the old model of rural rebellion, but with two dimensions added, namely social revolution (which is what the *Peasant Movement* Report is really about) and an ambitious ideology-governed objective. To put it more romantically, Mao was a mixture of Robin Hood, Lenin and Hung!

Ironically, Mao's analysis and subsequent decision put his family firmly into the upper peasant bracket, for as a member of the relevant committee he gave an acreage limit definition of the demarcation between rich and middle peasants well below his own father's holdings. Some idea of rural poverty is shown by the fact that even a well-to-do peasant family like Mao's subsisted largely on rice and vegetables (most of the meat and fish being reserved for working adults).

Some in the Party were critical, for various reasons, of the tough line taken in the peasant movement. For one thing, the policy of co-operation with the Kuomintang, endorsed by Stalin, meant that they needed to tread very warily since later in 1927 some of the Kuomintang leadership were to make the policy obsolete through the massacre of those Shanghai workers who had handed the city over to Chiang's advancing forces. Mao was at pains to rebut the attack on the movement, and it is in this context that he wrote the following famous lines:

A revolution is not a dinner party, or writing an essay, or painting a picture, or doing embroidery; it cannot be so refined, so leisurely and gentle, so temperate, kind, courteous, restrained and magnanimous. A revolution is an insurrection, an act of violence by which one class overthrows another. A rural revolution is a revolution by which the peasantry overthrows the power of the feudal landlord class.

Who is refined, leisurely and gentle and so forth? Mao is referring to the classical description of Confucius, and so of the gentlemanly ideal.

In looking at the essay I want largely to concentrate upon two issues: first, Mao's attitude to violence and other methods of coercion and persuasion; secondly, Mao's attitude to religion and the traditional ideology of the peasants. To open up the first of these topics, let us consider the various measures the peasant movement actually took.

Among the prohibitions the peasants imposed in the areas under their control were the elimination of gambling, the growing of opium and opium-smoking, vulgar shows, the use of sedan-chairs, distilling and sugar-refining, sumptuous feasts, vagabondage, and (in some districts) offerings for the dead. These puritan restrictions were designed to prevent in part the exploitation of people by those who cater for vices, and in part to signal a new social order – as with the destruction of sedan-chairs. All this was very reminiscent of the policy of the Taiping Revolution less than a century earlier. Many Taiping ideas had in the meantime gone underground, so one suspects some continuity.

The more 'political' methods (as Mao categorizes them) included dealing with landlords by the following actions: checking the accounts, imposing fines for past offences, levying contributions for poor relief, minor protests (such as sitting-in in a landlord's home, killing his pigs and having a feast), 'crowning' landlords with paper hats, and even gaoling, banishing or killing them.

As for more direct economic acts, the peasants enforced a prohibition on sending grain out of the particular area, increasing rents, etc., and on cancelling tenancies. Interest on debts was reduced. Since landlords sometimes had their own militia, these were disbanded and replaced by peasant irregulars to enforce their own rule. These then are some of the ways in which the peasants exercised coercion.

Obviously the most controversial aspect of these measures was the execution of landlords. This also happened in the course of the redistribution of land after 1949. Mao here makes two points. The first is simply that it was a matter of revenge – the 'evil gentry' often killed people somewhat casually and cruelly, so the execution of some landlords was a matter of appropriate revenge. Mao, optimistically, relies on the good sense of the peasants as to who are the worst landlords and so worthy of such severe punishment. Secondly, and more important, Mao saw such killings and other forms of violence as a way of liberating the peasants from the older attitudes of subservience.

This approach is relevant to the practice of 'crowning'

landlords with paper hats, with slogans and accusations written on them, and parading them through the village. This ritual performance is of course an act of public humiliation and was, according to Mao's account, much dreaded by the gentry: it was also a method much used in the Cultural Revolution thirty years later. Again the aim of these acts is to provide both catharsis and a new boldness for the peasants. Its psychological effects were of the greatest importance if the peasants were to realize that now a whole new order of society had been established. So Mao explicitly allows the use of violence, though it needs to be discriminating: terror is a necessary weapon.

This view of violence as an article of policy is disturbing. For someone like Mao to state that terror is a necessary instrument under certain circumstances seems somehow worse than casual violence – hot-headedness. Mao admittedly does not talk of the minimization of violence, which is in any view the correct aim in a bad world; but it would be unreasonable to expect him to eschew violence in a situation where his enemies relied on it to crush the peasant uprising. Mao was no Gandhi (perhaps China would have been better off if conquered by the British, instead of being simply beaten in the Opium War!).

In brief, as a revolutionary Mao acknowledged the use of violence, but he thought of it mainly as a means to effecting a change in the consciousness of the peasants. In all this he was defending the peasant movement, not acting in it. When he sanctioned killings it was chiefly, if not exclusively, in the course of warfare.

When we turn to look at his attitude to the religion and traditional ideology of the peasants we find a certain degree of 'naturalism'. By this I mean the willingness to let matters take their natural course. Mao regarded religion as superstition; but he knew that it had a strong hold over people – his mother, for example. He did not think that it was necessary to mount a frontal assault on religion, though the peasant themselves had done so where they saw it as a factor in their exploitation. Thus the peasants had taken over temples as schools and in some places smashed the images; but this appeared to be in areas where the peasants saw the religious system as reinforcing the economic and social system. About this connection and other elements of the traditional exploitation of ordinary people Mao wrote with some feeling:

> A man in China is usually subjected to the domination of three systems of authority: (1) the state system (political authority) . . . ; (2) the clan system (clan authority), ranging from the central ancestral temple and its branch temples down to the head of the household; and (3) the supernatural system (religious authority), ranging from the King of Hell down to the town and village gods belonging to the nether world, and from the Emperor of Heaven down to all the various gods and spirits belonging to the celestial world.

He goes on to discuss the subjugation of women, and this was one of his great concerns.

Though Mao spoke strongly against superstition, his general attitude was rather permissive. This was a sign of a certain confidence. He urged that the smashing of idols was not to be encouraged prematurely. He wrote:

> It is the peasants who made the idols, and when the time comes they will cast the idols aside with their own hands; there is no need for anyone else to do it for them prematurely.

On his own role in the propaganda against religion, he comments:

> Worship them (i.e. the gods) by all means. But if you had only Lord Kuan and the Goddess of Mercy and no peasant association, and you have overthrown the local tyrants and evil gentry? The gods and goddesses are indeed miserable objects. You have worshipped them for centuries, and they have not overthrown a single one of the local tyrants or evil gentry for you!

Mao was therefore keen to destroy religion, but he took a mild attitude towards it. This was probably because he considered it to be unimportant, or rather secondary. If the primary problems were solved, religion would wither away. By smashing what he called the state system and the clan system, religion would in effect be dealt with. Moreover, his work with the peasants in this period was seen by him not so much as the unleashing of a rural revolution as of the harnessing of it. It thus follows that religion itself would be destroyed spontaneously. Long afterwards he was to remark to André Malraux[1] : 'We organized peasant revolt, we did not instigate it. Revolution is a drama of passion; we did not win the people over by appealing to reason, but by developing hope, trust and fraternity. In the face of famine, the will to equality takes on a religious force.'

But there was to be considerable debate, up to the time of the Cultural Revolution, on the analysis of religion and the correct methods of treating it. This was partly because of the complex nature of Chinese religion itself. What is known loosely as Confucianism has two sides to it, on the one hand the philosophical and ethical teachings which instilled gentlemanly conduct and good order in society, and on the other the cult of ancestors ranging right up to the state cultus (discontinued effectively after 1911). From a practical point of view the ancestor cult was most important and pervaded Chinese society (except among minority groups such as Muslims and Christians). Next there was Taoism, which took on many magical characteristics as a rural religion. Then, highly important in Chinese spirituality, there was the whole phenomenon of Buddhism. These three religions of China blended together in a single system – but they could operate at different levels. For example, the Confucian ethic was specially prized among the feudal gentry and official class, while Taoism was largely a peasant cult; then again Buddhism has never excluded belief in gods and spirits – though it considers them irrelevant to the higher spiritual quest – so Buddhism could operate at the higher level and the other cults at a more worldly level. Moreover, though Buddhism can be represented as containing theistic elements in some of its manifestations (e.g. Pure Land Buddhism), it does not need the concept of God. It is mainly a non-theistic religion. This adds an extra dimension to the complexity of Chinese religion as perceived from a Western point of view – which inevitably meant that there were to be problems for Marxist interpretation. Marx (and his mentor Feuerbach) had been working with the assumptions of the West regarding religion. This meant that Marxism concentrated much on theism. This factor was important in the debate about religion which preceded the

Cultural Revolution.

From 1963 onwards this debate generated much discussion. This bears witness to the continuing importance of the issue. It seems that whenever controls were relaxed religious and magical practices cropped up again, even among some members of the Communist Party. It may be that in due course the party leadership and perhaps Mao himself became disillusioned with the Marxist prediction that religion would die out with the realization of a socialist revolution. However, we should note on this point that Mao's attitudes in the *Peasant Movement* Report owed more to his own feelings and observation than to Marxist theory.

This long debate was an attempt to clarify the situation created by the tension between Marxist orthodoxy and the Chinese situation. On the one hand, the theoretician Ya Han-chang took a relatively soft-line on religion. He was opposed by Yu Hsiang and Lin Chun-wang; and later by Fan Wen-lan, a leading Party intellectual and member of the Central Committee. Ya made a distinction between theistic belief, religion and superstition. This was not altogether a logical trichotomy, but no doubt some distinctions in a complex situation are better than none. All parties agreed that superstition was to be rooted out as being counter-revolutionary and unscientific. Theistic belief, too, was to be argued against, for it reflected an idealism fundamentally in conflict with dialectical materialism. Though religion was to be opposed, it should not be opposed by force as it would eventually die out because of its irrelevance. Ya was primarily thinking of Buddhism. However, party members were not unmindful of the fact that Taoism, through its tradition of anarchism and nonconformity to Confucian order, and through the secret societies associated with it, had contributed in the past to peasant rebellion and thus had helped to produce a foretaste of revolution. Neither were they, nor Mao, slow to realize that religious elements had been vital in the Taiping Revolution, and some were inclined to view the Taiping as a 'first shot' at what Mao later achieved. Chinese historians of the post-revolutionary period have been much divided about the Taiping phenomenon. Ultimately the debate was resolved in a definite manner, and virtually all outward manifestations of religious practice were eliminated at the time of the Cultural Revolution. Even earlier many of the ancestral tablets had been removed from temples, and this without a great deal of protest from the peasantry.

Does this mean, as some have argued, that Mao himself encouraged the attack on religious practice? I think it does, and that this represents a shift in his own thinking from the reliance on spontaneity and authority. In a way the issue goes deep into the whole meaning and viability of so-called 'democratic centralism' and the 'mass line'. Perhaps the point can be better put in symbolic terms, ones which Mao himself has used. He has more than once referred to the analogy between Heaven (the old Chinese concept of divine providence) and the People. There is little doubt that Mao is sincere in feeling strongly that the intuitions and feelings of the Chinese worker and peasant are essentially good. He is one of those who in ancient Chinese debate on the nature of man comes down on the side of the goodness theory. It is more a question of organizing these forces, and so in a sense manipulating the will of Heaven, than of artificially creating them. On the other hand, Mao's voluntarism and emphasis on the importance of the superstructure from time to time pulls in the direction of a strong-willed didacticism. Therefore, in the matter of religion one should, on the one hand, allow the good sense of the masses to destroy it as harmful and irrelevant, but yet, on the other, must interfere positively to accelerate the process of the spiritual liberation of the people from the superstitions and oppressive idealism of the past. In the end Mao's didacticism came out on top, and that, I suspect, is the real meaning of the debate between Ya and his victorious opponents. All this ultimately owed little to Marxist theory – it was only that Marxist theory, being part of the necessary furniture of the revolution, had to be taken account of.

It is interesting that when Mao's didacticism prevailed the methods were somewhat religious; that is, Mao has always paid attention to the ritual and symbolic aspects of events and to the inner experience and ethic which can be generated by the ritual dimension of human behaviour. This, as we have seen, is behind his endorsement of violence in the peasant movement in Hunan. Power may 'grow out of the barrel of a gun' – a remark which may sound cynical, but the true meaning of the aphorism is to do with power not guns. The latter can be thrown away in due course. So the true meaning of the execution of landlords is not to do with killing some so-called 'evil gentry', but rather to do with the irreversible change of attitude and feeling in the heart of the peasants. It has a ritual function.

This can be distasteful for by some quirk of the human soul we prefer killing to be unideological – dropping bombs by mistake on a village in Cambodia seems more acceptable than Aztec human sacrifice, and Manson seems more sinister than Bonnie and Clyde. Mao certainly defends ritual killing. Not for him the *crime de passion*.

To revert to Mao's analysis of the oppressed in the *Peasant Movement* Report, he referred to four forms of subordination – to the state system, the clan system, the supernatural system and to the male idea. Leaving aside the last, which Mao added somewhat as an after-thought, deeply as he came to believe in women's liberation, the first was seen as withering away, but there were religious and 'superstitious' factors involved with the other two. Traditionally the state system was supported by Confucian rituals, although this was no longer a problem under the Kuomintang and still less after the Communist take-over of China. As a result Mao does not comment on this aspect of religious traditionalism. On the other hand the clan system, in which was embedded not only Chinese traditional family life but also the social structure of rural China, was much reinforced by the ancestor cult. For this reason, a distinction seems to have been drawn in Mao's mind between Buddhism – the language of which he sometimes uses in his writings – and Confucianism. The latter had an ideology reinforcing the social system, while Buddhism at worst was a result of the suffering and alienated condition of the masses, a kind of opiate. The one was a positive ideology to be struggled strongly against, the latter a soporific which Mao at one time thought would no longer have effect after the awakening brought about by social revolution. As we have seen, he had become less certain of this last doctrine by the time of the Cultural Revolution.

To sum up on the *Peasant Movement* Report: it is an important study as it witnesses Mao's existential conversion to a mode of revolution based on the peasant movement, and also relates to Mao's basic analysis of the class structure in China and its relation to imperialism and to the possibility of re-creating the Chinese nation. Light is thrown on Mao's attitude to violence as a ritual act (for a revolutionary leader Mao's attitudes were relatively moderate – a point we need to discuss further in regard to his *On the Correct Handling of Contradictions among the People*), and it shows his view of traditional values including religion. As I have argued there seems to be a shift here from 1927 to the time of the Cultural Revolution. Later we need to consider how far Maoism has the capacity to replace the tradition of the three religions of China.

At the period when the *Peasant Movement* Report was written Mao had still only half-perceived the military aspect of revolution. However, he had a taste for military action and so it was not long before he was involved in organizing a rural military campaign in Chingkangshan and the surrounding areas, sometimes in defiance of party directions. We cannot ultimately separate Mao's theory of revolution from his theory of war, put most lucidly and forthrightly in his long essay *Problems of Strategy in China's Revolutionary War*, written in 1936, after the great events of the Long March and the establishment of a north-western base. Mao had absorbed a number of lessons and wished to resist mechanical and un-imaginative ways of applying military manuals and other inferences from military history not fitting the specific conditions of China.

Although simply, even crudely, stated, the essay is masterly. Mao's success partly stems from his ability to simplify complex situations and to put his finger on their main features. He is in the tradition of Chinese aphoristic writing. The West prefers qualification, accuracy, literal truth, whereas China prefers essences and practical deductions.

It is not necessary here to go into all the details of the essay – for much of it is an analysis of previous campaigns in Kiangsi. This is to show that if we do study the laws of war it must always be in context – too many generals fight the last war in the present. There was a tendency for the Chinese Communist Party to look to Soviet models of conducting civil war.

Mao analyses the Chinese situation as follows. First, China is a vast semi-colonial country which is unevenly developed. This unevenness makes for division, not only among the war-lords but between them and Chiang Kai-shek. Being semi-colonial there is another reason for disunity, namely disunity among the imperialist powers (eventually as we know they were to go to war against each other). Further, the vastness of

China not only gives it internal variety but also gives an army plenty of room for manoeuvre – as was well testified by the Long March itself. Mao states that characteristics of China need to be used in formulating Red strategy.

Secondly, the enemy is big and strong, for the Kuomintang had seized power and more or less stabilized its position by gaining the support of the principal imperialist states. Because it had called in foreign advisers and acquired a substantial store of guns and other war material, and because of a vigorous recruiting campaign, the Kuomintang was the biggest army in Chinese history. Mao is keen to point out that this means that the civil war in China was quite different from that in the Soviet Union.

Thirdly, Mao candidly concedes that the Red Army is weak:

Our political power exists in scattered and mountainous or remote regions and receives no outside help whatsoever . . . The Red Army is numerically small, its armies are poor and it has great difficulty in obtaining supplies such as food, bedding and clothing.

Fourthly, Mao emphasizes the Communist leadership of the agrarian revolution. On the one hand, even though the Chinese revolution was occurring in a period of reaction not only in China but also throughout the capitalist world, the base areas held by the Reds have great potential. On the other hand, the Kuomintang army is less stable, for the Kuomintang is against the agrarian revolution in principle. Its soldiers therefore could not believe in the cause for which they were supposed to be fighting. This last factor is the one which Mao seized on. The fact of rural revolution is all-important: it is the key both to military and to political success.

These observations of Mao in 1936 represent, then, a clarification of his views about the necessary pattern of a revolutionary war against the Kuomintang. The same pattern was to be used with modifications against the Japanese. Incidentally, Mao's concluding remarks in the essay are remarkably prophetic of the later phase of the Civil War. He remarks that most of the Red Army's supplies of munitions comes from the enemy. 'We have a claim on the output of the arsenals of London as well as Hangwang and, what is more, it is delivered to us by the enemy's transport corps. This is the sober truth, it is not a jest.' The war supplies pumped into China by the United States after 1945 helped to speed the collapse of the very forces the Americans were trying to support.

Thus, apart from Mao's own conviction of the revolutionary necessity of mobilizing the rural masses, he also saw the military necessity of having friendly peasants. Hence, the discipline imposed on all soldiers to treat the people honestly and correctly. The Red Army was not the devastating experience that other marauding armies had been in their roamings over the vast expanses of China.

In brief, both in his political and military thinking Mao had a clearer view of the possibilities in China than his rivals, whether inside the Party or amongst the enemy. The Kuomintang under Chiang unified most of the country, but at the expense of co-operating with foreign powers and internal capitalism. This was the reason for Chiang's marriage and his conversion to Methodism – a sop to America, which cherished until lately the dream of a Christian China – in Buddhist terms, a Pure Land to the West! The marriage between China and the Western powers was liable to be unstable for a reason which Mao clearly perceived. The Western powers and Japan, which had of course been admitted to the club, were in mutual conflict. That conflict could, and did, easily spill over into China itself. Further, the Kuomintang, despite its commitment to land reform, could only venture on this timidly, because of its alliance with some traditional forces. This is not to say that the Kuomintang did nothing; it was indeed an agent of change, but the change was more towards modernization than towards revolution, and that was not enough. Moreover, its élan was not high, its ideology was fuzzy, and it could not match the almost religious fervour of the Reds.

Mao saw this, and in due course saw too that an alliance with Chiang against the Japanese was not unfavourable to the Communist Party. If the Japanese won that would eliminate the Kuomintang and reduce the Communists again to an underground organization. If they did not, the base of Red power could be greatly expanded. Then the civil war could be fought on relatively favourable terms. The first hypothesis was a recipe for relative disaster, the second for absolute success. Mao therefore had his own Pascal wager.

Before leaving *Problems of Strategy*, there are one or two incidental points in it which require some comment, for they represent the seedlings of plants later to flourish in Mao's mind. Thus, he was already beginning to form some radical ideas about education. In the peasant movement in Hunan some new and exciting things were beginning to happen, such as evening schools for peasants. The original framework of Chinese education was the study of the Confucian classics and the use of such scholarly education as the basis of recruitment into the imperial civil service. So although theoretically one could go from peasant to mandarin, there was no real equality of opportunity because the mass of the peasantry could scarcely afford the time and tutoring for their children. Traditionally, therefore, the great majority of peasants were uneducated. However, the Kuomintang, and before them missionary societies and other agencies, were keen on a drive for literacy, and for this and other reasons schools were set up in many areas based on Western educational ideas. Mao himself had experienced this system, and was until the time of his *Peasant Movement* report an advocate of it. The enthusiastic, if perhaps naïve, drive of the peasants to set up their own classes, as distinguished from what they called the 'foreign schools', influenced him deeply. He was more impressed with motivation than technique or even content in education. He was drifting away both from the classical and the foreign ideals (even if the classical stayed with him in his poetry). Much later Mao was to be very radical about education in an almost aggressively anti-intellectual way. Thus, during the Cultural Revolution he is reported as having made the following remarks[2] when reference was made to schools which explain everything very thoroughly, in didactic detail:

That is scholasticism which is doomed to perish. Take the study of the classics for instance. So many commentaries, but they have all vanished. I think students trained in this method, be they Chinese, Americans or Russians, will perish, will negate themselves. There were many Buddhist sutras. The result of Hsuan-tsang's textual studies was one sutra of just over 1,000 words. There were also those sutras by Chiu-mo-lo-shih – very wordy. They have disappeared, however. The *Five Classics* and the *Thirteen Classics* cannot find readers any more.

One must not read too much. Books by Marx should be read, but not too many of them. A few dozen volumes will do. Too much reading will lead you to the opposite of what you expect to be, a bookworm, a dogmatist, a revisionist. Confucius's scholarship does not include industry and agriculture, hence 'the four limbs are not laboured and the five kinds of cereals unrecognized'. This must be remedied.

From the *Peasant Movement* report onwards, there was always a strong flavour of practicability in Mao's thinking. Here, he is caught in a trap of his own making. The fact is that he has tended to dogmatize on educational and cultural matters, but he has dogmatized against dogma. He has tried, no doubt quite sincerely, to liberate people's thinking by getting them to be critical and realistic about both traditional and Western methods of education; but the new freedom has to be exercised in a Mao-inspired straitjacket. The hundred flowers can bloom provided they are not blue or white or purple or yellow – they must all be cheerfully red. However, this may be part of the bitter and ironic price to be paid for the evangelical recreation of Chinese society through establishing a new heaven and a new earth. The five kinds of cereals grow better than the hundred flowers.

Another important, though subsidiary, point in the *Peasant Movement* report is Mao's early emphasis upon women's liberation. Again he was echoing something in the Taiping programme, but it is still rather remarkable in terms of the Chinese tradition. Thus he writes:

As for women, in addition to being dominated by these three kinds of authority (i.e. the state system, the clan system and the supernatural system), they are also dominated by the men (the authority of the husband). These four authorities – political, clan, religious and masculine – are the embodiment of the whole feudal-patriarchal system and ideology, and are the four thick ropes binding the Chinese people, particularly the peasants.

Mao has from these early days felt very strongly about women's liberation, and Chiang Ching's prominent place in central policy-making (especially in regard to the Cultural Revolution) is a neat combination of dynastic solidarity and theoretical egalitarianism between the sexes.

To sum up: much of Mao's thinking and practice are to be found in this very practical and influential report. It is the seminal moment in Mao's development of a rural and military, essentially Chinese, revolution, within the framework of his own reading of Marxism.

6 Mao on new democracy

Mao's *On New Democracy* dates from 1940. Though the Reds were well entrenched in the north-west and displaying vigour in the war against Japan, the situation as a whole was somewhat depressing. Yet there is little sign of this in the confident and lapidary language of *On New Democracy*. The occasion of its publication was the first issue of a new periodical called *Chinese Culture*, so theoretically it is directed to discussing culture – but mainly it is political and historical in its emphasis. About culture Mao is modest : 'I am a layman in matters of culture; I would like to study them but I have only just begun to do so.' He goes on to emphasize that his remarks are intended to be scientific, and he welcomes discussion and criticism. (However, 'the only yardstick of truth is the revolutionary practice of millions of people.')

Much in *On New Democracy* defined the relationships of Chinese communism to other types of revolution and society. Mao has a clear set of distinctions, for example, to clarify the difference between the Chinese Marxist approach and the doctrines of the Kuomintang. Thus he considers Sun Yat sen's famous Three Principles and their interpretation. These, it may be recalled, are the following : the Principles of Nationalism, Democracy, and People's Livelihood. The Communists must go beyond the bourgeois democratic revolution which was the aim of Sun (and something which he partially achieved). First, that revolution is to be succeeded by the socialist revolution. Secondly, democracy needs concrete economic implementation, by a thorough redistribution of land and ultimately collectivization; an eight-hour day must be introduced; rights for people in their work must be safeguarded. These measures, Mao points out, go well beyond the usual Kuomintang interpretation of the Principles.

There is something a bit artificial in bouncing the eight-hour day into a definition of general policy, but Mao ruggedly persists in seeing social revolution and national independence as two sides of the same coin.

Secondly, Mao stresses that the Kuomintang had a minimum

programme of democratic revolution, but the Communists a maximum programme, right through to the stage of communism. Thirdly, the Kuomintang principle of People's Livelihood, though correct in what it was seeking, is not seen in global political terms and so was not in line with dialectical materialism. Finally, and rather significantly in terms of Mao's own temperament, their actions belie their thoughts. Theory and practice have to be kept together.

In brief, Mao shows why the Reds could quite sincerely embrace the framework of official Koumintang intentions while regarding them as only one stage in the overall strategy of Chinese revolution. How far is Mao's analysis of the Chinese Communist strategy, in its relation to world revolution and the October Revolution in Russia, something which he was obliged from an official Marxist point of view to affirm, and how far was it something in which he really believed? In all his writings the least plausible parts are those concerning the Soviet Union, and it was perhaps for this reason that he was so shocked at himself and at the Soviets over the decision to break with them, and the causes of that break. We shall later see some of his feelings as expressed in poetry on this point. I think Mao was sincere in all he said about alliance with the Soviets, even if his experience of the agents of the International and of Stalin's advice regarding China led him early on to think that the USSR could be pretty fallible in matters of policy. Of all the agents perhaps the Indian Roy showed the greatest appreciation of the special condition of China. But the record, from Mao's point of view, was poor, and he must have known that Stalin's support for the Chinese Reds was, to put no finer point on it, lukewarm. Mao was never a sycophant or a man to mince words: writing about Lu Hun he says that he was 'a man of unyielding integrity, free from all sycophancy and obsequiousness; this quality is invaluable among colonial and semi-colonial peoples . . . on the cultural front he was the bravest and most correct, the firmest, the most loyal and the most ardent national hero, a hero without parallel in our history.' He admired toughness and pride, qualities which he himself so conspicuously displayed. It is likely that Mao really believed in the Soviet connection. Without hiding the fact that Stalin could be out of touch with Chinese realities, Mao went out of his way to quote him with approval from time to time in his writings. It is not surprising that he should have been cheerful in pointing to the Russian Revolution and confident of the internationally solid nature of the Communist movement, for it was early days in the International and even as late as 1940 Mao could still look on his own conversion to Marxism as relatively recent. So he still retained the freshness of his ideological enthusiasm; but given all this, we should note that he very definitely went his own way. We shall see further proof of this as we continue to explore *On New Democracy*.

The definition of the Chinese Communist Party's difference from the Kuomintang, though a vital element in *On New Democracy*, is less significant than Mao's general remarks about the distinction between the new democracy in China and other systems of government and aims of revolution. Thus he writes as follows:

> This new democratic republic will be different from the old European-American form of capitalist republic under bourgeois dictatorship, which is the old democratic form and already out of date. On the other hand, it will also be different from the socialist republic of the Soviet type under the dictatorship of the proletariat which is already flourishing in the USSR, and which, moreover, will be established in all the capitalist countries and will undoubtedly become the dominant form of state and governmental structure in all the industrially advanced countries. However, for a certain historical period this form is not suitable for the revolutions in the colonial and semi-colonial countries.

During this period the new-democratic form will be appropriate for these countries, says Mao. But why? And how did he conceive of the difference between the Soviet model and the incipient Chinese one?

Part of Mao's reasoning depended upon an estimate of the international system which proved to be on the whole mistaken. In 1940 he could be forgiven for thinking that liberation and social democracy – the main flowers produced by bourgeois 'dictatorship' (he really means control) – were on the way out. The Nazi and Fascist phenomena were more gripping and powerful for the distant observer. They also conformed to Marxist theory. Mao was not then to perceive that the bourgeois democracies would not only come out on top but spread their system to some of the major world nations, such as Japan and India. He is reported to have said, at the time of the rapprochement with Nixon, that he preferred a Nixon to a Kennedy – for with liberals you were never quite clear where you stood. If he did say something like this it indicates an uneasiness in giving up democratic liberalism. Anyway, in 1940 Mao thought that liberalism was dying. But this of course was not his main interest, for the question of the difference between the Chinese and the Soviet models was a more lively issue, since liberalism was never in Mao's view a live option for China, as it required a strong and independent, national bourgeois basis.

The distinction between the two models lay in the difference of the classes involved in controlling or dominating the respective systems. This is consistent with the whole of Mao's thinking. For on his analysis the Chinese revolution in effect telescoped the bourgeois, democratic, and social phases of the revolution, in that there is an alliance between the proletariat, the peasants and some important elements of the bourgeoisie. He speaks of a 'democratic republic under the joint dictatorship of all anti-imperialist and anti-feudal people led by the proletariat . . .' Of course Mao was, in 1940, laying the theoretical basis of a continuing co-operation with the Kuomintang. But he was also more importantly claiming that the classical first phase of revolution – the bourgeois-democratic – would not in fact be predominantly bourgeois. This in turn led Mao to a rather different theory of the socialist stage of the revolution, which would be organized politically on the system of democratic centralism. This was no doubt a somewhat contradictory conception, except that it testified to Mao's continuing belief in the essential goodness and right-mindedness of the Chinese people. One could dictate to them, but only in accordance with their essential feelings. The people replaced Heaven: the ruler follows the way of the People.

In the course of articulating his theory for the first time Mao gives a fully worked out statement of the preceding stages of recent Chinese history. Once again we see the importance of May 4th, 1919. It is almost Year One of a renewed China in Mao's thinking. The first stage, then, is from 1919 to 1921, the date of the foundation of the Chinese Communist Party. Mao considers that May 4th was the beginning of a conscious call for revolution; and even if this was not fully informed, nevertheless a number of intellectuals and students had some rudiments of Communist ideology. The second period was from the foundation of the Party to the split with the Kuomintang in 1927. Mao writes quite warmly of the co-operation with the Kuomintang, and even more so of Sun Yat-sen: he 'was a great man not only because he led the great Revolution of 1911' (although it was only a democratic revolution of the old period), but also because, 'adapting himself to the trends of the world and meeting the needs of the masses', he had the capacity to bring forward the revolutionary Three Great Policies of alliance with Russia, co-operation with the Communist Party, and assistance to the peasants and workers. Mao singles out as significant two elements in the revolutionary activity of this period, the reform of the army with Soviet assistance culminating in the victory of the Northern Expedition, and the attack on Confucianism and classical education and literary style.

The third period was the decade from 1927 to 1937. This was of course the time of the Kiangsi Soviet and the encirclement campaigns against the Reds, which was followed by the Long March. The divisions within China were one main reason for the belief among the Japanese leadership that it might be possible to conquer the whole country. Sufficiently serious was the threat for the Kuomintang and the Reds to agree to co-operate in the anti-Japanese war.

The fourth period started in a lively and courageous spirit, but after the fall of Wuhan, according to Mao's account, things became more depressing, with some of the bourgeoisie favouring capitulation, and some actually co-operating with the Japanese who had set up a puppet government. How was it all going to end? Even in the dark days in 1940 Mao spoke optimistically. What great changes China would see in the next twenty years.

The whole tone of Mao's discussion at the political level is relatively moderate. The same applies to his views of cultural developments. To these I shall come in a moment, but in the meantime it is worth seeing how realistic Mao's outlook was. For he was not given to a revolutionary rashness but always stressed that the revolution would come about as events ripened. This was the basis both of his optimism and of his middle path within the context of Left politics. Throughout his writings there is a surprising consistency in his analysis of

Chinese historical trends.

At the cultural level Mao naturally addressed himself to the question of how to treat Western ideas. China still had quite a number of advocates of wholesale westernization. This was very natural in a period when the Japanese who had appeared to do this very thing were militarily dominant. But, as Mao remarks in a famous passage:

> We should assimilate whatever is useful to us today not only from the present-day socialist and new-democratic cultures but also from the earlier cultures of other nations, for example, from the culture of the various capitalist countries in the Age of Enlightenment. However, we should not gulp any of this foreign material, but must treat it as we do our food – first chewing it, then submitting it to the working of the stomach and intestines with their juices and secretions, and separating it into nutriment to be absorbed and waste matter to be discarded – before it can nourish us. To advocate 'wholesale Westernisation' is wrong. China has suffered from the mechanical absorption of foreign material. Similarly, in applying Marxism to China, Chinese Communists must fully and properly integrate the universal truth of Marxism with the concrete practice of the Chinese revolution . . .

Mao also implied that Marxist ideology would play the leading and formative role in a new democratic culture.

This echoes an urgent plea he had composed in the latter part of 1939 entitled *Recruit Large Numbers of Intellectuals*. By intellectuals are meant those with high school or higher education. There had been a tendency for the peasants and workers to ostracize intellectuals during the Agrarian Revolution and Mao himself had a somewhat ambivalent attitude to formal education. Though he perceived clearly that an educated élite was necessary as part of the leadership, he was always disturbed by the possibility of the intellectuals lapsing back into bourgeois habits. As we have already seen, there was a strong element of deschooling in his thought. Perhaps, too, there were deep psychological roots to his ambivalence. He had done much in the pursuit of education, himself, as a youth and young man. He was stubbornly determined to learn as much as his circumstances permitted. Yet this led to some tension with his family, and notably his father, with whom he was often in conflict. Here was a tug-of-war between his peasant origins and his intellectual ambitions. In one of the few autobiographical passages in his writings he wrote:

> I began life as a student and at school acquired the ways of a student . . . At that time I thought that intellectuals were the only clean people in the world, while in comparison workers and peasants were dirty. I did not mind wearing the clothes of other intellectuals, believing them clean, but I would not put on clothes belonging to a worker, believing them dirty. But after I became a revolutionary and lived with workers and peasants and with soldiers of the revolutionary army, I gradually came to know them well and they came to know me well too . . . I came to feel that compared with the workers and peasants the unmoulded intellectuals were not clean and that, in the last analysis, the workers and peasants were the cleanest people and, even though their hands were soiled and their feet smeared with cow-dung, they were really cleaner than the bourgeois and petty-bourgeois intellectuals.

The latter, he goes on, will be misfits unless they remould their thinking.

These remarks were made in the context of a forum at Yenan on literature and art in 1942. He had become increasingly interested in the theoretical issues about literature and the other arts, and was quite heavily influenced by Lu Hsün in the direction of a more direct equivalence between literary and spoken styles. In brief, he was moving away, in theory, from the classicism which still informed his poetry. Certainly his own prose is often very direct. It must not be forgotten that in the previous forty years great upheavals were occurring in the whole Chinese literary scene, and for that matter in the other arts, although the most dramatic problems were literary, partly because of the nature of the Chinese language and scholarly tradition.

Lu Hsün was perhaps the central figure in the literary revolution which, though foreshadowed before the May 4th Movement, really came into being in its wake. The difficulty with the preceding literary and scholarly tradition was fivefold

– and all this was relevant to Mao's struggle to promote a coherent view of the arts. First, the literary tradition was on the whole deeply entangled with Confucianism because of the role played by the classics in the imperial examination system. As Mao says 'In my childhood I never attended a Marxism-Leninist school and was taught only such things as The Master said "How pleasant is it to learn and constantly review what one has learned." Though this teaching material was antiquated, it did do some good because from it I learned to read.' Thus a revolt against Confucianism involved a revolt against the older literary style. Secondly, the fact that the literary tradition was élitist meant that a new style was needed in order to realize a democratic literature. Thirdly, the actual nature of the Chinese language, with its largely non-phonetic, aphoristic and allusive character system was always liable to open up a gulf between literary and ordinary language that was much deeper than that found in any natural language. Hence quite a lot a thought has gone into the whole problem of language reform. Thus the Communists have brought in a system of simplified characters (annoying for those who knew the old and have to learn afresh) and are in the long term thinking in terms of romanization. Fourthly, the older style was not easily adapted to the importation of new and technical terminology. Just as many centuries earlier Sanskrit words were transliterated into their rough Chinese equivalents with disastrous effects on their meaning – rather like the English soldier who translates Bar-le-Duc as Barley Duke, Yprès as Wipers and Béthune as Bay-tune – so in the early years of the century democracy could become the meaningless *te-mo-k'o-la-hsi*, the name for a certain variety of foreign magic. Fifthly, the older tradition encouraged a stereotyped approach to literary production. The strictness of the so-called eight-legged essay was notorious : an essay had to include a presentation, an amplification, a preliminary exposition, an initial argument, and then four different sequences of paragraphs, the last three having contrastive sections (i.e. each being two-legged). Lu Hsün and other writers were breaking through this rigid formalism.

It can be seen that the problems confronting the modernization of Chinese literary style were in part cultural, in part political and social, and in part structural. Of these the structural aspect was the least troublesome, even if there are, for example, great technical difficulties about romanization. Nor perhaps was there too great difficulty about overcoming the stereotyped cultural heritage. However, it is significant that Mao devoted the better part of two essays to the problem of a new form of stereotype. It is not surprising that many Party intellectuals should see Marxism and its jargon as a substitute for the older style. Mao is very schoolmasterly in his lecturing of his erring pupils on this matter. However, the really big question concerned the relation of a literary élite to the masses. This at any rate was as Mao saw it: politics and art needed to be fused.

It can hardly be said that his prescription was likely to be unconditionally successful, at least not in terms of the individualism and creativity which characterize modern literary work. It is true that in regard to non-conforming creativity there was no need, certainly from Mao's point of view, for China to follow Western literary techniques and ethics with their necessarily bourgeois orientation. But there was a contradiction between the freedom of spirit shown by Lu Hsün and other literary reformers and the populist conformism which Mao's prescriptions were likely to produce. There is evidence that Mao himself has remained somewhat worried and puzzled as to how a good literature is to develop in post-liberation China. The hundred flowers did not cheer him, nor do popular stories inspire him.

What then were Mao's prescriptions? First, that literature should be directed at the audience of workers, peasants and soldiers. In brief, it was to be directed at a particularly unsophisticated audience, especially in the context of China in the early 1940s when the level of literacy remained low. Hence the forum in Yenan also considered the whole problem of raising standards. So, secondly, universal education must perfect literacy and teach correct outlooks; of course, here was the flaw, for though in principle the Party encouraged criticism, and Mao attacked conformism and dogmatism, the cards were bound to be stacked in favour of ideological rigidity so long as art was geared to utilitarian party ends, and the same applied to education.

In an interesting passage he refers to utilitarianism. He was here no doubt drawing on his youthful reading of John Stuart Mill, whose writings influenced Mao as they did other Chinese intellectuals of his generation. Mao writes as follows:

> Materialists do not oppose utilitarianism in general but the utilitarianism of the feudal, bourgeois and petty-bourgeois classes . . . We are proletarian revolutionary utilitarians and take as our point of departure the unity of the present and future interests of the masses.

However, Mao well stated the problem which has not yet been solved in Red China. Referring to a famous ancient story of two songs, one of high standard and the other of great appeal, he wrote:

> The question now is to bring about a unity between 'The Spring Snow' and 'The Song of the Rustic Poor'.

How? Mao was perhaps rather Ch'an (that is, Zen, to use the more familiar Japanese form of the word) in his optimistic belief regarding the possibility of fusing populism with the raising of standards. It will be recalled that Zen involves an extraordinary attempt to use control and discipline to bring about a spontaneity in life and religious experience. This is symbolized by methods such as training in archery to bring about the higher spiritual experience. Thus a well-known book by Eugen Herrigel called *Zen in the Art of Archery* describes the way in which a Zen master teaches his pupil to hit the target without aiming. In brief you can attain your target with entire spontaneity, like singing in the bath. The paradox has a certain earthy realism in any event, for those who aim at happiness usually do not get it (not that aiming at unhappiness is any good!), but still there are controllable conditions for happiness. Mao seems to have thought that creativity is possible within a highly constricted and disciplined framework. And the history of art and literature tells us that this is not an unrealistic notion, except for one thing. It is not for nothing that we see a qualitative difference in modern political ideologies, namely their being totalitarian. This means a form of thought control that is very pervasive. Of course, some arts can be pervaded more easily than others – literature, art, opera more than music, pottery and perfumery. So there is a real question as to whether the modern phase, following upon the establishment of the reality of totalitarianism, is one in which the Zen principle can work. The literary and artistic output of post-liberation China does not encourage optimism in the possibility of regimented creativity.

Much of Mao's interest in the problems of literature and the arts was fairly new during his Yenan period. It arose partly from the stimulus of reading Lu Hsün, who had died in 1936 and who was the subject of a commemorative address by Mao in the following year. There he referred to Lu Hsün as a modern saint and praised him for his revolutionary zeal, fortitude and courage. If Confucius was the saint of ancient times, Lu Hsün was the one for the modern age. The point would not have been lost on his audience, for Confucius was not merely the sage but also the prime model of Chinese scholarship and literary tradition. So Mao was presenting a new stylistic model.

This had an effect on his own style. In the first period of his writing Mao had been fairly classical and conservative. His two theoretical works, *On Practice* and *On Contradiction*, displayed strong traces of Marxist jargon and the influence of European philosophical language. But in the period from the late 1930s onwards Mao became freer, pithier and not only more given to colloquialisms but also more ironic and humorous. This was part of his drive to get his comrades to write in a less contorted style. Their task was difficult in that Party intellectuals were trying to apply a foreign ideology, woodenly translated and fairly heavily steeped in jargon anyway. Also, Mao's newer style may have been encouraged by the enthusiasm of his second wife, who always displayed a strong interest in cultural developments. However, the changes in Mao's prose style did not affect his use of classical forms in his poetry.

Thus by his example and exhortation Mao helped to loosen the grip of Marxist fundamentalism on Party intellectuals, both at the level of ideas and of stereotyped language. Even so, a brief glance at such a publication as the *Chinese-English Glossary of Current Affairs, Words and Phrases*, published in Peking, is sufficient to show that plenty of stereotypes remain – including the stereotype that stereotypes have to be removed. In other words, ultimately Mao's thinking about the role of intellectuals and culture has not been markedly successful. Mao's military thinking has been, by contrast, remarkably so. To that I now turn.

7 Mao on War

Mao's military doctrines have proved influential beyond China as they may be applied by the organization of guerilla campaigns in a Third World context. A substantial proportion of his writings is devoted to military matters, partly because of Mao's romantic involvement with war. He was of course widely read in military history. Probably the most important of his writings in this area was *On Protracted War*. But in what follows I shall also draw upon his *Problems of Strategy in Guerilla War against Japan* and *Problems of War and Strategy*.

His *On Protracted War* was written in 1938. The war with Japan had been in progress for nearly a year, and though it was clearly going to be a long struggle, Mao showed a lapidary confidence in ultimate victory. This is clearly expressed in his answers to Edgar Snow, which are in part reproduced in *On Protracted War*. The basis of this confidence was that, because of the size and populousness of China, the Japanese would be overwhelmed and ultimately destroyed. He may also have heard something of the current Japanese debate on whether the Empire should 'go south', that is, dominate the south-west Pacific by occupying Indonesia, Malaysia and South-East Asia, since he predicts this. Later on in *On Protracted War* Mao was to predict also the spread of warfare in Europe which would make the war global. It was as well, for the Japanese war would indeed have been very protracted without the introduction of US technological warfare.

However, Mao's Marxism did not always provide realistic answers to problems. He was overconfident of a Japanese revolution in the long run. Thus one of the three conditions for the success of his struggle was, he averred, the rise of the revolutionary movement of the people of Japan and the Japanese Colonies. It is true that history appeared to favour the hypothesis, since war-weariness and military defeat triggered off revolutionary insurrections in Russia, Germany and elsewhere. However, these may only partly be described as class revolts, since they were deeply affected with the very sentiments fuelling war, namely nationalism: revolutions are a mode of restoring national identity. Naturally, left-wing insurrection is likely, in that the Left's ideology provides it with a theory and a leadership of those who are most likely to rebel, namely those who suffer most, such as ordinary soldiers and the urban poor. But fascist and rightist insurrections are also possible, because they promote a virulent nationalism. Be that as it may, Mao considered that the contradictions in Japanese society would ultimately betray themselves. The victorious Allies had some such theory also, for the basis of pumping aid into Germany, Italy, Japan and so on was to forestall the possibility of leftist insurrections. Can Revolutions be drowned in spaghetti, noodles and wurst? A generation after cataclysmic defeat nationalism can go on the rampage once more. Hence, this is, after all, the reason for the recent nervousness about Japan exhibited by the Chinese leadership, as Japan begins to throw its economic weight around and to leave American tutelage. Beyond the GNP there looms the rising sun, dawning afresh, a galling sight for the Chinese who have had to struggle to a weaker position.

However, Mao's analysis of the respective strengths and weaknesses of China and Japan was otherwise largely accurate. First, Japan was not only one of the half dozen foremost imperialist powers, but in particular was the first in the East. The contradictions of her political and economic structure led her to embark on a very ambitious war : according to Mao the military-feudal character of Japanese imperialism led to its peculiar barbarity (no doubt he was thinking of the rape of Nanking and other atrocities). However, Japan's population and resources were not in his view sufficient to sustain her in a long war. Further, while Japan might be able to get support from the fascist countries, she would attract strong international opposition so that her enemies would outnumber her friends. Mao writes :

To sum up, Japan's advantage is in her great capacity to wage war, and her disadvantages lie in the reactionary and barbarous nature of her war, in the inadequacy of her manpower and material resources, and in her meagre international support. What, by contrast, about the Chinese side of the equation?

Reiterating his preoccupation with the study of recent

M   C

Chinese history, Mao points out that the Opium War, the Taiping Revolution, the Reform Movement of 1898, the Revolution of 1911 and the Northern Expedition of 1926–7 all had their reverses. The Opium War was of course a straight defeat, the Taipings eventually broke up under Manchu pressure and internal problems; and, as we have seen, the Reforms of 1898 were short-lived, the Revolution of 1911 gave way to the neo-imperial pretensions of Yuan Shih-kai, and the Northern Expedition led to the split between the Kuomintang and the Reds, with Chi'ang going towards the compradors. So, although the Chinese giant was awakening, it still had not recreated itself and was therefore still weak. However, the waves of the Chinese revolution made it increasingly progressive; although weak it had the future on its side – 'China is a country like the rising sun.' In other words, China's war was a just war (Mao often stressed that there are no reasons for rejecting war, only for rejecting unjust war: just war in his view would lead to world peace for ever, eventually – the problem being: how long does 'eventually' imply? We shall come back to Mao's view about the future of the world in due course). The other side of the Japanese coin is that China would win wider international support in its struggle. 'To sum up,' he goes on, 'China's disadvantage - lies in her military weakness and her advantages lie in the progressive and just character of her war, her great size and her abundant international support.' These were the underlying factors to be remembered, and any superficial military assessment would fail unless it took these factors into account. Once again Mao looks at things simply.

Mao felt certain that the major characteristic of the developing war would be its jigsaw pattern. Though there had been other jigsaw pattern wars in history, notably in the post-revolutionary civil war in the USSR, China's would be the greatest and longest and most celebrated. What Mao had in mind had to do with his division of operations into three sorts, the positional, the mobile, and the guerilla forms of warfare. The main emphasis was to be on the latter two forms. The distinction between them I shall come to in a moment. But both are typically forms which involve piecemeal and fluid attack rooted in the base areas.

The Japanese, on the other hand, as the superior and occupying force, would attempt to occupy the cities and the lines of communication. Even so there would be hundreds of base areas behind their lines – hence the jigsaw effect. The distinction between mobile and guerilla forms of warfare was largely a matter of scale and recruitment. The idea was to use the regular Red Army (and for that matter the Kuomintang forces if possible) for mobile strikes typically on interior lines. When a weaker army confronts a stronger it is an elementary consideration that it can by concentration achieve greater strength than some parts of the more powerful army. So the object is to swallow those parts piecemeal, mainly by logistical flexibility, deception and surprise. But a big meal cannot be swallowed at once. And the extraordinary power of the Japanese army would mean that the 'banquet' would indeed take a very long time.

Guerilla warfare, however, was more irregular and 'grass roots' in character. If the peasants were properly organized they could be both the fish and the sea of operations against the enemy. The detached guerilla areas would mean that the guerillas operated on exterior lines. By co-ordinating the two methods it would be possible to grind units of the enemy in a double way.

With this Mao sets the scene for the long-drawn-out combat with Japan. We may note that his preference from an early date was for guerilla warfare, partly because of his romantic admiration for the déclassé bandit chiefs who were the Robin Hoods of his early novel reading, and who indeed helped him in his early days in Chingkangshan. Indeed, his position was originally near that of the 'Guerillaism' which he later condemned. What he came to perceive as a result of his military experience was that one could in China combine guerilla warfare with substantial base areas, which need not in the last resort be defended by positional warfare if it proved unprofitable. This was because of the sheer size of China. Indeed the whole warlord period demonstrated the difference between Chinese and modern European warfare. In China war was conducted more on the older pattern of armies wheeling through large areas, occasionally colliding and fighting pitched battles. Hence base areas, mobile regular warfare and guerilla warfare; such was Mao's general prescription in the fight against the Japanese. Quite obviously it relied on political factors (war indeed is politics with blood, and political power grows out of the barrel of a gun): the strategy would not only have no point without a long-term political aim but would have no chance. For the guerilla strategy itself depended heavily upon peasant support; national sentiment and agrarian reform would have to go hand in hand. This was a reason for Mao's confidence, for neither the Japanese nor the Kuomintang could command the degree of rural support that the Reds had. This meant that the collapse of Japan would leave the Reds with a strong grip on a whole series of rear areas, mainly in the north of China.

From these more particular concerns about the nature of the Japanese conflict Mao proceeds to some general observations about war which illustrate his own conception of it as a human enterprise. As we have more than once remarked, he is something of a military romantic, seeing war as something very central both to his own and to other men's experience of life. Many of his family had died in the bloodshed, as well as many friends and comrades. We shall later see something of his feelings about death. But war, if tragic, was, like the best of games, also noble. Yet ultimately it would issue in perpetual peace. Thus he wrote:

> This war . . . will be greater in scale and more ruthless than the war of twenty years ago. But, owing to the existence of the Soviet Union and the growing political consciousness of the world, great revolutionary wars will undoubtedly emerge from this war to oppose all counter-revolutionary wars, thus giving this war the character of a struggle for perpetual peace. Even if later there should be another period of war, perpetual world peace will not be far off.

Mao was thinking along the same lines later when he was to introduce the spine-chilling thesis that 'reactionaries and atom bombs are paper tigers'. As he remarked (referring probably to a conversation with Pandit Nehru): 'I debated this question with a foreign statesman. He believed that if an atomic war was fought, the whole of mankind might be annihilated. I said that if the worst came to the worst and half of mankind died, the other half would remain while imperialism would be razed to the ground and the whole world would become socialist. In a certain number of years there would be 2,700 million people and definitely more.'

I suppose from a utilitarian point of view, if you are confident that this outcome would ensure perpetual peace, and, within the limits of a continuing permanent revolution, happiness, the calculation is justified. But Mao was being rather theoretical and overconfident in thinking that socialism and peace would prevail. The Russians were somewhat shocked by Mao's line on this – and of course he was later to lose his optimism that the USSR was a socialist society.

At any event, the paper tiger thesis was part of Mao's military voluntarism. For in *On Protracted War* Mao has a section of great importance called 'Man's Dynamic Role in War'. Here he especially directs his remarks to commanders, with the revealing words 'the stage of action for commanders in a war must be built upon objective possibilities, but on that stage they can direct the performance of many a drama, full of sound and colour, power and grandeur.' Not for nothing was Mao an admirer of Napoleon. Hence, also, Mao's continuing emphasis upon a correct political understanding as the framework for military strategy, for only if the commander had that basis could he 'swim in the ocean of war' and only if the troops understood their objectives would they fight effectively. The relation between war and politics is explained by Mao as a qualitative one. When politics develop beyond that certain point where policy objectives can be achieved by the usual processes, war breaks out to sweep the obstacles out of the way.

Some of Mao's remarks on the technical problems of warfare throw light on his conception of political organization – he has sometimes in later years expressed the analogy between political actions and a campaign. Thus in his *Problems of Strategy in Guerilla War* he refers among other things to the problem of guerilla command. An absolutely centralized command in guerilla warfare is a contradiction in terms. On the other hand, there must be some kind of central direction. How is the problem to be resolved? Mao suggests that one can make a distinction between the overall strategy and particular battles and engagements (this is not precisely the distinction between strategy and tactics); and so there can be a centralized command dealing with the former, while local junior commanders plan their own coups of various kinds.

There is an obvious analogy between this and the semi-anarchistic ideas involved in Mao's interpretation of democratic centralism. For this division was, for example, one attraction of the commune as a unit of organization. In this way the central committee of the Party might dictate strategy, and handle foreign policy and so on, while the masses could take their own decisions in a piecemeal and decentralized manner. Some observers of contemporary China have remarked on the apparent success of this policy in practice. However, we shall be returning to the evaluation of Mao's later ideas.

Before we leave Mao's thinking on war, it is worth remarking on his power of clarifying issues. This may make his analysis rather obvious, but that is a commodity often in short supply among military thinkers. Generals are usually fighting some previous war. Indeed, perhaps Mao himself falls into this trap in thinking about nuclear warfare, though even here one sees his unrelenting toughness of thought. Mao had read a lot of theory and history on military matters, but he also had the advantage of being an amateur. That meant he could start off afresh, and try to work out his military programme in the modern Chinese context. The sort of coherent clarity he achieved is well represented in the following from *On Protracted War*:

In ancient warfare, the spear and the shield were used, the spear to attack and destroy the enemy, and the shield to defend and preserve oneself. To the present day, all weapons are still an extension of the spear and the shield. The bomber, the machine-gun, the long-range gun and poison gas are developments of the spear, while the air-raid shelter, the steel-helmet, the concrete fortification and the gas mask are developments of the shield. The tank is a new weapon combining functions of both spear and shield. Attack is the chief means of destroying the enemy, but defence cannot be dispensed with. In attack the immediate object is to destroy the enemy, but at the same time it is self-preservation, because if the enemy is not destroyed, you will be destroyed . . . It should be pointed out that destruction of the enemy is the primary object of war and self-preservation is secondary, because only by destroying the enemy in large numbers can one effectively preserve oneself . . .

Thus it is clear that Mao evolved a clearly and simply articulated theory of war in China, given the concrete conditions of the particular time and place. By a mixture of courage, intuition and good fortune he was able to put his theories into practice. He was helped in this by a number of tough and brilliant associates, notably Chu-Teh, Chou En-lai and the ultimately ill-fated Lin Piao. But all great generals and leaders need good luck and Mao was no exception.

As for the theory – or perhaps one should say the spirit – animating Mao's military thinking: the most important aspect was the human factor, which meant right politics leading to cultivation of good morale because of the popular and nationalistic character of the politics, plus dynamic leadership. That was how the leaders of the revolution could swim in the sea of war.

8 Mao on cultural revolution

We have now surveyed and commented on some of Mao's major writings, and must turn to his later years and consider the extraordinary changes and upheavals which were in large measure due to his own initiatives. It is impossible to give a full estimate of Mao's thinking without transcending the classical writings of the *Selected Works*, for Mao's theoretical mind works itself out in social practice, a point he was always very keen to stress himself.

Here we enter into an area of speculation, for it is not always clear how far Mao's thinking has entered into such upheavals as the Great Leap and the Cultural Revolution, since Western observers still have much to discover about these events. However, I shall be assuming that to a great extent these events did in fact reflect Mao's ideology. There is, for example, little doubt that the episodes in question, and others such as the Hundred Flowers, represent Mao's own belief in the necessity of a permanent or continuing revolution. Of these upheavals one was cultural, another was economic, and the third essentially political (but all had secondary aspects). The Hundred Flowers was a crusade for freedom of thought; the Great Leap was an attempt to merge country and city in a new synthesis with an accent on high production; the Cultural Revolution was an attempt to redirect the management of the country and to break down the incipient alienation between the Party bureaucracy and the masses. Of these episodes the Cultural Revolution was, of course, the most ambitious.

Among the miscellaneous writings of the period is the 1957 *On the Correct Handling of Contradictions among the People*, actually the written version of a speech delivered in June of that year. This develops the idea of non-antagonistic contradictions and contains a strong plea against the use of violence in the settlement of ideological disputes. We have already seen that Mao's theory of a perpetual revolution is bound up with his whole philosophy of the centrality of contradictions in the evolution of nature and society. In this essay he also examines the particular contradictions in a socialist society : a reaffirmation, in some degree, of the anarchistic tendencies latent in his thinking. Thus in listing them he refers to, among other things, contradictions between the government and the masses.

These include contradictions between the interests of the state, collective interests, and individual interests; between democracy and centralism; between those in positions of leadership and those led; and contradictions arising from the bureaucratic practices of certain state functionaries in their relations with the masses.

As usual, Mao was struggling with the old problem of trying to instil spontaneity by order, and of trying to command some loosening of the bureaucracy and of democratic centralism. This was preparatory to his ultimate aim, which was to induce young party members to attack the Party apparatus itself in the events of the Cultural Revolution. To that we shall return.

In his emphasis on non-antagonistic contradictions, Mao even goes so far as to say that an antagonistic contradiction can be turned into a non-antagonistic one if it is properly handled. Thus the contradiction between the national bourgeoisie and the workers is in theory of the former kind but is open to such transformation. So, for instance, we must 'unite with, criticize and educate the national bourgeoisie' in a peaceful way – and they for their part need to accept their education. Therefore what was required was a gigantic pedagogical exercise. But though Mao frequently speaks of criticism there are severe limits on the development of a critical attitude (in, say, the Popperian sense), for democracy and freedom are always within the bounds of socialist discipline. Even if questions of right and wrong in the arts and sciences are said in one passage to require settlement through free discussion in artistic and scientific circles, Mao is careful elsewhere to lay down six criteria for judging words and actions – the two most important being their following the socialist path, and recognizing the leadership of the Party (a criterion later to be modified).

Mao is, however, firmly committed to the view that ideological struggle has its own particular form. It is not one where crude and coercive methods can be used, but rather persuasion and pressure. If there is an analogy with the West it can be seen in the process of evangelism – preaching, teaching, appealing, pressing. Mao remarks that in the ideological struggle in China socialism has strong advantages, for the Communist Party is in control and its prestige stands high. Also, remarking on the Hundred Flowers, Mao says that even if you ban the expression of wrong ideas, the ideas will still be there. In this as in other matters, and more spectacularly in the unleashing of the Cultural Revolution itself, Mao recognizes disturbance as inevitable, though he discourages violence.

Incidentally, Mao's express concern in these later writings with rigidity in the state and Party machine has been a major reason for his appeal to certain left-wing elements in the West in the last few years. Combine this with his being the foremost actor and theoretician in Third World revolution, and so in a revolution which includes Vietnam, and Mao could easily be a symbol of leftist libertarianism. But such interpretations of Mao as go under the name of Marxism in the West tend to be eclectic. Despite his anti-bureaucratism Mao demands a considerable degree of conformity. He is not a *libertarian* anarchist: it would be better to see him as a Marxist populist. Thus he thinks that his democratic centralism is possible in large part because the workers and peasants have fundamentally sound ideas if these can but be brought to light – and fortunately these correspond to Maoist doctrine in the last resort. It is, if you like, an evangelism of the inner light (an inner red light!) which the cadres and Red Guards can espouse. This is brought out in the following passage from the directive *Some Questions Concerning Methods of Leadership* issued by the Central Committee of the Communist Party in China in 1943, written by Mao:

In all the practical work of our Party, all correct leadership is necessarily 'from the masses, to the masses'. This means: take the ideas of the masses (scattered and unsystematic ideas) and concentrate them (theory and study turn them into concentrated and systematic ideas), then go to the masses and propagate and explain those ideas, until the masses embrace them as their own, hold fast to them and translate them into action, and test the correctness of these ideas in such action.

Then those ideas are taken again, reconcentrated, and so on in an endless spiral.

However, later on Mao was to have a rather different and more Olympian thought. In an article published in 1958, he wrote:

China's 600 million people have two remarkable peculiarities: they are, first of all, poor, and secondly blank. That may seem like a bad thing, but it is really a good thing. Poor people want change, want to do things, want revolution. A clean sheet of paper has no blotches and so the newest and most beautiful words can be written on it, the newest and most beautiful pictures can be painted on it.

He goes on to commend the use of large character posters, as if these slogans were what was being written on the blank paper of the Chinese people's mind. Interestingly Mao also quotes a poem on the Ch'ing dynasty:

Let thunderbolts rouse the universe to life . . .
Alas that ten thousand horses should stand mute!
I urge Heaven to bestir itself anew
And send down talented men of every kind.

The inner meaning of the poem is quite clear. Here, as elsewhere, for Mao Heaven is the Chinese people. So Mao calls on the people to stir itself and to produce talented leaders.

This of course has been a profound problem for the leadership, for the heroes of the Long March and the Liberation are ageing or dead. How can democratic centralism cope with the need for younger leaders at the centre? Chou En-lai himself somewhat wistfully remarked on the relative youth of the senior administrators surrounding Nixon on his Peking visit.

Mao's mood in the above remarks on the Chinese people varies somewhat from his earlier populism but nevertheless has some continuity with his whole doctrine of perpetual contradiction and struggle, for that itself implies an indefinite possibility of transforming human nature and society. But Mao has increasingly felt the problem of time: he feels all could yet be lost if different forces take over and do not press forward with the task of transformation. This was the occasion of the Cultural Revolution.

Part of the success of that great upheaval lay in the thorough reshaping of education, for since the leadership would inevit-

ably be drawn from among the intellectuals – and many
students continued to have petty bourgeois attitudes – it might
be possible to ensure the continuation of the revolution as a
proletarian revolution. Not for nothing was it called the Great
Proletarian Cultural Revolution. Mao, in one of his pronuncia-
mentos of the time, could say that the workers should run the
schools forever, and that in the countryside this should be
done by the poor and lower peasants. In any event, since the
aim of the revolution was to revolutionize people's ideology (as
the carefully tailored resolution of the 1966 meeting of the
Central Committee which launched the affair declares) it was
not at all surprising that a major aspect of its work should be
in education. Here Mao was increasingly radical: 'It is still
necessary to have universities: here I refer mainly to the need
for colleges of science and engineering. However it is essential
to shorten the length of schooling . . .' and he could make
disparaging remarks about book learning, as we have noted.
This iconoclasm was combined with a desire to force intellectuals to work in the countryside and the factories, and thus
to break down incipient élitism. Again it was a romantic
vision.

Another aspect of Mao's attitudes of this later period was his
distaste for the consumer societies – whether Western capitalist
or the goulash communism of Eastern Europe. Of course there
had always been an element of austerity and toughness in
Mao's makeup: in his early years he deliberately set out to
toughen his physique – an emphasis on physical culture which
was to stand him in good stead in his hardy adventures, and
which also helps to explain the craze for physical exercises
permeating modern Chinese society. There was hope that
by emphasizing a decentralized commune-based semi-rural
economy, the problems of pollution and urbanized ugliness
might be overcome. Though in many matters Mao was indebted
to Lenin he did not follow him in a fanatical concern for heavy
industry. Shifting the industry into the countryside is more
useful than shifting the peasant into the town, as happened
in most other industrializing countries, including the USSR.
In his more romantic moments Mao's voluntarism and accent
on human dynamism came to dominate: it was better to be
Red than expert.

In all of this the split with the USSR must have played a
deep part in Mao's thinking. As we have seen, Mao was sincere

in his solidarity with Stalin even if he frankly stated his mistakes. From his early years as a Marxist he was committed to the alliance with the Soviet Union, and a cardinal point both in his faith and in his optimistic analysis of developing world history was the fact of the Russian Revolution. Of course, he was shaping a Chinese Marxism which was not identical with Marxist-Leninism, but even if he maintained this ideological independence and resisted a mechanical application of Marxism to China, this does not mean that he failed to recognize warmly his Marxist, and more particularly Leninist, heritage. So the split with Russia was a traumatic one – to think that the birthplace of the Revolution should become the cradle of social imperialism and Kruschev's bureaucratic revisionism! It is not surprising that Chinese anti-Soviet propaganda became shrill. How was the Soviet backsliding to be explained? Again, it is probable that Mao was genuine in seeing it as a horrid example of what he feared might happen in China. In this context the Cultural Revolution is an expression of the need for perpetual struggle against those forces within a socialist society leading to a state bourgeois ethos. The event led to a paradox : as China's internal policies became more radical, so the logic of its new international position led to a new less radical posture. First it was largely a posture of withdrawal and effective isolationism, but beyond that, in the period after the upheaval, it meant a relaxation of revolutionary ideals in foreign policy. Maoism, as a result, became less and less for export and more and more a Chinese ideology which might perchance be imitated. China was beleaguered, so a rapprochement with the USA would do no harm : but it was in another respect the Central Kingdom once more, for it could be the highest expression of the new humanity. I shall return to this when considering Mao's 'religious' role.

Therefore, in his later years, Mao has given a certain concreteness to the idea of persisting contradictions, and has at the same time become preoccupied with the project of utterly transforming Chinese humanity. The real question is whether his educational theory can actually work : what will happen when flowers are allowed to bloom again? Moreover, Mao has not really solved the contradiction inherent in the democratic centralism which has characterized his theory of leadership.

One last general point. When Mao said that political power

grows out of the barrel of a gun it was in the context of the need to keep political control of the gun itself; in other words, the Party must rule the army. It was a big gamble in the Cultural Revolution to issue the slogan 'Bombard the Headquarters' (i.e. of the Party) for Mao might have fatally weakened the political control of the military. As it turned out he had to let the army arbitrate in the later phases of the Cultural Revolution. Perhaps Mao was just lucky that in time Lin Piao overreached himself.

So Mao turns his back on the past, with successive waves of revolutionary ardour. That is one reason why he does not attach much importance to his poems; they belong to the old style, no longer genuinely relevant in the transformation of socialist society. Still, the poems tell us something of the man. To them we now turn.

9 Mao's poems

Mao's thought is not directly related to his poems. Yet although he is modest about them (most have not been published and some discarded), they have a sharpness and intensity which reflects his way of seeing and feeling the world. I do not claim to be a literary critic, least of all of works in Chinese, a language which few Westerners fully grasp, but these few remarks may help to relate his poems to his ideology. In quoting them I shall use Michael Bullock and Jerome Ch'en's versions from the latter's *Mao and the Chinese Revolution*.

It is remarkable how many of the poems are about mountains. 'Yellow Crane Tower' introduces the Snake and Tortoise Hills, by Wuch'ang; the next poem is 'Chingkang Mountain'; 'New Year's Day 1929' centres on Wuyi Mountain; 'Huich'ang' speaks of the green hills and peaks of the Kiangsi-Fukin borders; 'March on Chian' refers to crossing a mountain pass; 'The Second Encirclement' is partly about White Cloud Mountain; 'Loushan Pass' is about a bitter mountain battle; 'Three Short Poems' all concern mountains; 'The Long March' is largely about mountains; 'Mount Liup'an' is about Mount Liup'an; 'K'unhun' is about the Karakoram range; 'Lushan' is about Mount Lu; 'Reply to a Friend' begins with Mount Chui-yi; 'Inscription on a Photograph of the Cave of the Immortals, Lushan' is also about Mount Lu. This amounts to sixteen out of a total of thirty-six. A large part of Mao's epic struggle was in the hills and mountains, and from a young age he liked to walk in the mountains, so for him they came to symbolize the tough struggle (he is not sentimental about nature, but happy to accept both its beauty and its harshness) and a certain Olympian view of events. There is a Buddhist image of the wise man who is on a mountain: the mass of men are in the plains: it is the wise man who can see far. So in Mao's mountain fighting he was both struggling and seeing, beyond the vision of most of his contemporaries. The poems also contain a sense of the immensity and mysteriousness of China – and nowhere is this clearer than in his famous 'Snow'.

The poems tend to romanticize warfare, one of Mao's great

loves. The blood and the hardships only appear as incidentals,
as in 'Tapoti':

> A desperate battle
>   raged here once.
> Bullet holes
>   pit the walls of the village
> They are an embellishment
> And today the hills
>   seem yet more fair.

Since in few of the poems is there a sense of repose, it is fair
to say that they combine some elements of Mao's three out-
standing characteristics: physical hardiness, perpetual struggle,
and fascination for warfare. Even in 'Lushan', which can be
read as a kind of nostalgia for future peace, he is actually
stating the opposite:

> Who knows where Magistrate T'ao has gone?
> Could he be farming in the Land of Peach Blossoms?

The peace of T'ao is introduced with a question mark. It is not
so much that, as Bullock and Ch'en say in their note (p. 351),
the poem delineates the author's longing, as he looks out from
the mountain over the China he loves, for peace in a turbulent
age. His mythological allusion here is not unlike his reference
in 'Yellow Crane Tower' to the quest for immortality. A saint
who attained immortality is supposed to have flown by here
on a yellow crane, mythologically the bird of immortality.
Mao writes:

> The yellow crane
>   has departed.
> Who knows where it has gone?

This is compatible with immortality being somewhere, just as
in the other poem peace might be sometime, but essentially
deathlessness and absolute paradise are not for us in a world
of everlasting struggle.

Many of Mao's personal poems are sad: he looks back to
the death of his wife – the one he had loved, admired and
wooed in Peking, and who was captured and beheaded a few

years later, in 1930. In 1957 he wrote a poem for his old friend
Li Shu-yi, whose wife Liu (being a CCP member and woman
fighter) was killed in the battle of Hunghu in 1933. Mao's wife's
name means poplar and Li's willow. Hence:

> My proud poplar is lost to me
>   and to you your willow;
> Poplar and willow
>   soar to the highest heaven.
> When they asked Wu Kang
>   What he had to give them
> He presented them
>   with cassia wine.
>
> The lonely goddess
>   who dwells in the moon
> Spreads her white sleeves
>   to dance for these good souls
>   in the boundless sky . . .

Wu Kang had tried to get the elixir of life, immortality, but
he was condemned to cut down an evergrowing cassia of the
moon. The wine is itself the ambrosial drink. The goddess
Chang stole the elixir and fled to the moon, but is lonely. The
whole poem indicates ambiguity. Incidentally, Mao's wife
refused to renounce him when captured, and it was for this
she was beheaded. Mao's sister was executed at the same time.
Who would not write a poem for such dear loyalty? But the
poem is not bitter – Mao never moans about hardship nor
becomes embittered by personal losses. He is sometimes fierce
about the enemy, but this is controlled violence. He has tended
to be restrained in violence and rational in his use of force.
This indicates a certain active serenity, and this reflects itself
in many of his poems.

Some of his later poems show a certain nostalgia, as in
'Return to Shaoshan'. He is glad to see the village he left
thirty-two years before, but there is a little sadness too.

> I curse the time that has flowed past
> Since the dimly-remembered dream of my departure . . .

Lofty emotions were expressed in self-sacrifice
So the sun and moon were asked to give a new face to
    Heaven.

In delight I watch a thousand waves of growing rice and
    beans,
And heroes everywhere going home in the smoky sunset.

His nostalgia is proud in the saga of the reformation of the
people, but always behind this is the urgency of the perpetual
revolution. Thus in his reply to Kuo Mo-jo (1963):

There have always been
Many things that were urgent.
Although the world spins on
Time is short.
Millennia are too long:
Let us dispute about mornings and evenings.
The four seas are tempestuous as clouds and waters
    show their wrath . . .

And this in the time of the Sino-Soviet dispute. But his basic
optimism remains:

In this small world
A few flies knock against walls.

Mao's poetry bears witness to his wider vision: a man on a
mountain, not complaining of the cold and weariness, only
seeing the snow sparkling and the vision of the great land of
China, now in blood and green beauty, tomorrow in struggles
and fields of waving, but not alien, corn.

10 Mao as a religious leader

The analogy between Maoism and religion has often been made. In one respect the matter is one of definition, but it can be illuminating to look into the comparison because it can help indirectly to explain certain aspects of the development of Mao's thought. So let us begin at the level of definition and then see how far the analogy applies. Here I rely on an analysis of religion which I have used elsewhere.[1]

The analysis involves treating religion as a six-dimensional phenomenon. These six dimensions are: the doctrinal, the mythic, the ethical, the ritual, the experimental and the social or institutional. I will expand on these in turn, but one can note initially that the first three have to do with beliefs and values; the second three to do with human experience and behaviour.

By the doctrinal dimension I mean a religious web of beliefs, as systematized. The doctrines give the anatomy of the universe and the relations between men, nature and the transcendental realm. However, at another level these relations may be inter-connected with various kinds of non-historical and historical events. Therefore, another level is the mythic, for myths (and history-based myths are included here, such as the story of the life, death and resurrection of the historical Jesus) are *stories* of the relationships between men, nature and the transcendental. Next, in the light of the doctrines and myths a religion will possess a web of social and ethical beliefs. They may involve attitudes which flow from the central doctrines and myths: for instance, the Christian is supposed to have attitudes of love and humility since these are believed to be characteristics of God and of Christ's life.

As for the practical side of religion, religions involve rituals, such as worship and prayer. These help to express and evoke religious sentiments and experiences, such as devotion and awe. Most dramatically, such experiences culminate in prophetic visions and mystical states. A religion must also inevitably have some rudimentary social institutions to carry on the rituals, maintain the beliefs, and articulate the life of the faithful. Typically such institutions are far from rudimentary.

These then are the six dimensions of religion. It is little more than a heuristic grid, but I think it is a fair framework. How does Maoism fare if matched against this grid?

First, of course it has an articulated and authoritative set of doctrines. It is true that typically religions involve reference to the transcendent or supernatural, and yet Mao's doctrines are this-worldly. Still, there is a certain transcendence of the empirical in the flavour of his teachings. Thus, the notion that behind the appearances there lie dynamic contradictions has an analogy to some religious ideas in China's own past such as the interplay of the Yin and the Yang and the voodist doctrines of the Mahayana. After all, whether the ultimate lies above or deep down within things is more a matter of taste in metaphorical directions than a solid distinction. However, it will be necessary to come back to the question of the Chineseness of Maoism later. But to sum up: the doctrinal dimension is, obviously enough, represented in Maoism even if the concept of the 'beyond' is somewhat different and in ethos earthly. Secondly, Maoism has its mythology. The moving picture of the dialectical forces operating through recent Chinese history is close to being mythic in the technical sense. Moreover, Mao very explicitly talks of the Long March not only in romantic terms but as a kind of manifesto, a proclamation of revolutionary power. That is what historical myth is – a proclamation on the basis of historical (or supposedly historical) events. Not that Mao himself would see things like this: very often myth is most powerful for those who only unconsciously know it as myth but consciously treat it as literal truth. Where Mao is conscious of myth it is in his poems and he has a theory of it. In a way, therefore, it functions not as myth but as mythology. Thus he writes:

> Although stories of endless metamorphoses in mythology and nursery talks can delight people because they imaginatively embody man's conquest of the forces of nature and, moreover, the best mythology possesses, as Marx put it, 'eternal charm' yet mythology is not based on the specific conditions of actual contradictions and therefore does not scientifically reflect reality.[2]

But of course secretly science in the sense understood by Mao (who tied it in with Marxism and failed to associate with it genuine criticism and scientific methodology – and what is science but a result of method and the method or methods involved?) was itself a kind of breeding-ground of the mythical, under the signs of the doctrinal.

Thirdly, the social and ethical beliefs of Maoism flow from its doctrinal and mythic dimensions. It provided a substitute for the old Confucian tradition. Mao himself writes of the May 4th Movement of 1919 that one of its slogans was 'Down with the old ethics and up with the new', and he and the Party certainly paid much attention to inculcating a radically new system of behaviour.

As for the other three dimensions, it is certainly true that there has been at different times a varying emphasis on ritual. At the height of the Cultural Revolution an important part of the ritual consisted of the carrying and raising aloft of the so-called Little Red Book. You can tell whether a text is sacred or not by seeing what can and cannot be done to it. Standing on a copy of the Little Red Book would not have been a safe thing to do in the streets of Canton or Ch'angsha! Further, in the course of rectification campaigns there have been ritual humiliations, confessionals, etc. The singing of patriotic and revolutionary songs, marching at rallies and so on, all these are part of the necessary ritual of Chinese Communism.

Ritual expresses and evokes certain kinds of experiences. It is true that the Chinese phenomenon does not include much in the way of numinous awe – though perhaps for some people the cult of Mao induces something very like this. The most central experience in the Maoist context is conversion. Time and time again people testify to their conversion away from selfishness and incorrect ideas towards an exalted service of the masses in the name of the Party. Further, the Maoist ideology gives people – according to the pious accounts published *pour encourager les autres* – a sense of faith and power which enables them to overcome all obstacles. Hence, Mao almost becomes a miracle-worker – when amazing operations are successfully conducted, great afforestation plans concluded, heroic rescues undertaken, complex engineering problems solved, all by the application of Mao's thought. Admittedly, such cultic phenomena have lately been moderated: perhaps Mao fears the final irony of socialist superstition, having himself destroying feudal superstition.

Finally, it is clear that Maoism has its institutions to carry on the teachings, whether notably in the Party, or also cadres outside the Party, and the Red Guards. Mao's chief problem, as we have seen, has been how to keep the institution flexible and relatively open to changing conditions.

So, if we match Maoism against the religious grid it fits quite well. The reason why we may *not* think of it as a religion is that it is professedly anti-religious. But there are different ways of being anti-religious and – if I may be Irish about it – one way is the religious way. When the Conquistadors destroyed the Aztec power they destroyed their idols and system of religious practice. Naturally, they did this in the name of their own religion, but from an Aztec point of view Christianity was very far removed from their traditional conception of religion. The very militancy of Maoism in the face of the religions of China, culminating in the closing of temples, etc., during the Cultural Revolution, exhibited what I may call a religiously anti-religious zeal. This is very different from the humanist temper, which wants to replace religion by something which would certainly not match up to the grid which we have used. Sacred rituals, authoritative books, evangelical morality, all these would fade into non-existence in a humanist world. Maoism is not that world.

Moreover, Maoist eschatology provides a kind of substitute for the transcendental. If there is no heaven for the individual, there is a mysterious ultimate transformation of humanity. But typically, as with most eschatologies, no limit in time can be put on this, for the date is indefinitely in the future, perhaps infinitely.

If the analogy with religion is successfully drawn, then we can with benefit use some of the experience gained from the history of religions to analyse Mao's past and prospects.

First, the whole phenomenon of the impact of Western religion, culture and technology upon non-European societies has shown some fairly consistent patterns of interplay and reaction across this frontier between two worlds – a frontier which I shall refer to as the White Frontier. The effects have initially been rather disruptive, especially in relatively small-scale societies such as the American Indians, the various peoples of Africa and so on; but the shock along the White Frontier has been fairly severe in larger societies with a sophisticated and long-living cultural tradition. If we see what happens at the smaller level first it will help to illuminate some features of the large-scale situation. The disruption of a society involves a wounding or death of the gods: the older social values and customs cannot cope with the influx of ideas, goods and people from across the White Frontier. Since very often the invading forces also include missionaries, one solution of the weaker society is to take over the white man's ideology. That, at least, involves an alternative discipline and framework of social stability. However, in a generation or two there are liable to be outbreaks of some new religious form – often part Christian – but attempting to recreate some of the older values and to restore ethnic consciousness. Hundreds of such new religions are found in Africa.

However, for various reasons a small-scale group may be relatively resistant to Christian belief. Here you are liable to get a new indigenous religion, such as the Ghost Dance among the North American Indians, and then a generation or two later Peyotism – a more successful religion for the recreation of Indian values.

The large-scale societies have been relatively resistant to Christianity. Naturally some converts were made, for instance in India and China, for that was one option of borrowing from the foreign culture. However, the invading culture was itself plural – one could accept, for instance, democratic liberalism or Marxism. The latter had the advantages of modernity for in effect the need for modernization was the problem of such societies. As with small-scale societies there is a crucial difference between this and adopting a reshaped native ideology. If a society is not too thoroughly disrupted, it can get away with revamping its indigenous tradition and blending it with a degree of Westernization – compare the recent histories of India and China.

In India the disruption was not too severe, for India has always been polycentric and pluralistic – it is less easy to shatter a bunch of grapes than an egg. It could indeed capitalize on this polycentricity, and present a new, world, version of Hinduism as embracing in principle all forms of religion. This new universal religion was a departure, but one which started firmly within the ambience of India's ancient and medieval tradition. For various reasons, notably the long-standing recognition of the need for tolerance in a variegated society, this ideology could marry quite well with democratic liberalism.

By contrast, China, despite not being conquered and completely carved up by foreign powers, was effectively disrupted both by the effects of the Opium War and the Taiping Revolution, and by the later warlordism. This was partly because Chinese society was administratively centralized, and in part because the older Confucian ideology was the ideology of the centre. Once this edifice had been broken in 1911 there was a real question as to what could replace it. Sun Yat-sen made a concerted attempt at synthesizing a set of values which combined Western and Chinese constitutional and social thinking, but it was not highly doctrinal and mythic. Experience indicates that where a society is fairly disintegrated and chaotic it is more likely to borrow its ideology from outside. The egg is fertilized from outside and the grape grows from its own pip: of the available options Marxism was the obvious choice.

But such an ideology had to be adapted to the Chinese scene, without losing its hermeneutical legitimacy – that is, without seeming too far from original orthodoxy. This was Mao's intuitive achievement, the sinification of Marxism while believing in his Marxist legitimacy.

One reason why Marxism was the obvious choice for China was because it could function with the same assumptions as the religious heritage of China, part of which had provided the ideological cement for a centralized system. The mandate of Heaven could stay, the People being the new god.

At this point it is worth glancing at the relation between Maoism and the Chinese tradition. As I have remarked earlier, it is foolish to see a direct continuity as though Marxism is Neo-Neo-Confucianism, as some lovers of the old China have optimistically concluded. It is more in the nature of a quantum jump from the old or, to put it another way, Maoism has to fulfil a function analogous to the old religious culture's function, and it has at the same time to reject the old. I shall call these two aspects respectively analogical function and content reversal. Why was content reversal necessary?

Novelty has two virtues in those circumstances when the values and ideas which have sustained you are failing and you need new ones. Usually they do not fail too drastically so you can build on the past – this is modification and adaptation: it is progressive but not revolutionary. But if your values fail badly, you need rebirth, and must start all over again. This helps to scrap what is now useless and is at the same time psychologically attractive. The person who fails needs the assurance of recreation – to turn over a new leaf, as we say. So both objectively (from the point of view of the national failure of the old ideology) and psychologically, content-reversal was useful and attractive: 'Down with the old ethics, up with the new!' More particularly from the standpoint of China's deepening national and spiritual crisis, content reversal could be important in ways related to the three strands of Chinese religion. Let us deal with these in turn.

First, Confucianism – what were its weaknesses? It was largely the ethic of the gentry and official classes, in a situation where the whole system of government was changing. Further, Confucian education did not equip officials to understand modern science and the practicalities of China's new situation. As for its expression in ancestor-cults, this hindered the reformation of China's family structure. Mao was strong in his attack on this structure partly for the romantic reason that women should be liberated and equal (Mao was a 'women's lib' advocate before its time) and partly because women could be a new source of labour: the crèche 'frees' women for the factory floor. But, in addition to all this, and perhaps most importantly of all, Confucianism did not have a strongly worked out world-theory. True, there has been a sophisticated Neo-Confucianism, but in the main Confucianism of the modern period was not vital in its *Weltanschauung*, and a condition of an ideology's success is that it plausibly relates cosmic forces to human existence. The existential force of a theory lies in its love bond between the macrocosm and the microcosm, and a religion needs existential force. This was withering beside the elegant pools in which latter-day Confucianism was reflected and among the courtyards of the imperial palaces, where intrigue and ignorance stored up débâcle.

What of Buddhism? It was in one way a curious opposite to Confucianism. It was strong on cosmic theory, where Confucianism tended to be weak, and so it was existentially successful, both at the intellectual and the less sophisticated level. It had Ch'an and the Pure Land. However, it had two disadvantages; first, it only intermittently had state support, and it was often despised by the upper classes. As a result of this heritage it was less well adapted to be the ideology of a nationalist China – and we must never forget that China was smarting under hurts and bitten with the nationalist bug, which loves to fly across the White Frontier. Though there was a modest revival of Buddhism in the 1920s and 1930s it was too peaceable to form the militant backbone of a new China. Only in Japan had they managed, with Nichiren and Zen, to create violent Buddhists. Mao loved his mother who was a pious Buddhist – and on the whole has taken a soft line with Buddhism. His *Little Red Book* is a new *Lotus Sutra*, understanding one sentence of which would guarantee salvation – but he has not taken it seriously. Mao is no pacifist and China's position needed warfare for independence, not a Gandhian figure.

Taoism in its original mode was anarchistic, and Mao once in his young days proclaimed himself an anarchist. But the main thirst of Taoist and Buddhist popular religion was magical. This aspect was bound to crumble in front of the new magic represented by Western science and medicine. Thus Taoism was scarcely a modernizing force. Since one of the deeper problems of Chinese culture of the last hundred years has been the power generated by the apparently inferior West through the applications of science, the future ideology of China needed to weave a scientific strand into its fabric. Marxism rated well on this even if in some respects Mao's interpretations of science are profoundly unscientific. Yet very often an ideology works by giving the sense of 'A' even if it does not really mean 'A': thus, moralists are often not moral, and those who stress higher moral standards often unknowingly betray the spirit of morality. To return to anarchism – this could hardly work as a Chinese imperative in the face of powerful external forces: it would have to be such powerful anarchism that it would be centralized. China was not Catalonia. The anarchistic tradition had lived on, however, in the secret societies, which were often active in peasant revolts and more random banditry. Mao was able to use such sentiments, but they had been (except among the Taipings) largely undirected.

Other religions had even a lesser part to play. Islam, though important, was a minority faith in Western China. And Christianity, despite American missionary dreams, was scarcely destined to control the soul of China, partly because it did not control the soul of the West and partly because it could not solve the problem of nationalism. Since it was largely 'establishment' Christianity – whether Anglican, American Baptist or Portuguese Catholic – which penetrated China, it was too entangled with the forces of imperialism to function strongly enough as a catalyst of nationalism. Not for nothing did Chiang Kai-shek become a Methodist. Marxism, by contrast, was cheerfully and powerfully anti-establishment in the imperialist nations. It hated what the Chinese saw as their enemies. Further, Marxism seemed more scientific than Christianity.

In brief, content reversal was needed. How could this be worked out? Against Confucianism – a proletarian and peasant ethic. Against Neo-Confucianism – materialism. Against ancestors – liberation from clan and male dominance. Against the archaism of the Yin and the Yang – dialectics. Against seeking stability in the past – historical development and revolution. Against gentlemanliness – toughness. Against Buddhism – national warfare. Against meditation – action. Against the doctrine of Karma – historical necessities. Against reincarnation – popular solidarity and class analysis. Against monks – cadres. Against Buddhisattvas – the suffering proletariat. Against Taoism – science. Against anarchism – democratic centralism. Against secret societies – the Communist Party. Against the quest for immortality – the indefinite interplay of contradictions and the transformation of humanity.

So much then for the content reversal in Maoism: what about the analogical function – how does Maoism fare here? Let us again take the three traditions.

Confucianism at the state level implied a theory of government and an ethos for the élite who implemented that government. The theory centred on the Emperor's mediating the will of Heaven, but this was controlled by the ultimate recognition of the principle *Vox populi vox dei*: the mandate of Heaven could well be withdrawn. Marxism fits this conception reasonably well, for it provided a theory of government (the dictatorship of the proletariat) which could be given a populist interpretation. Further, it could provide an ethos for the substitute for the mandarinate, the Party and the cadres (Mao's Cultural Revolution is a recognition of the danger of the mandarinization of that élite). The new élite of course is not an equivalent but an analogy for the old. The danger is always that analogies collapse into the literal.

At the local level Maoism had to provide a functional analogy to the old family system. This was part of the meaning of the commune, the work brigade and other collective groups tried out in the post-liberation period.

As far as Buddhism goes, Maoism's functional analogy is the cultic attention to his own person, which has some resemblance to the devotionalism of the Pure Land school and some other Mahayana sects. But further, Buddhism was very much the higher religion of the lower classes. It provided an eschatology which had as its analogical function the proletariat-peasant oriented vision of the future, to some degree realized in the present through the reforms of the post-liberation period. Also, Buddhism was the great metaphysical religion of China: functionally, Marxism provided a new metaphysics.

Taoism supplied anarchy, and a need at the grass roots for magic. The functional analogy in Maoism is first the genuine if regimented decentralization – the syndicalist streak in Mao's thinking – and second the palpable material results of the new ideology, at least for some.

Will the content reversal and the analogical function ensure Maoism's survival in China? We have of course left out the religious and ethical problems of the individual. Death strikes my child, not humanity nor even the Chinese people at large. This is an aspect of the functioning of religion as an existential force unduly neglected in Mao's writings (except perhaps in his poems in one or two places). This is one main reason for a certain scepticism about the ultimate success of Maoism's religiously analogical function.

What then of Mao's future? Is he becoming dated? I doubt it. His intuitive grasp of the realities of the Chinese situation made him a charismatic leader, and as such he has been both prophet and maker of the new China. Yet what does his charisma consist in? And what are its inevitable limitations?

Mao's charisma lies partly in his military and political success – his toughness and confidence. But from the point of view of his ultimate grasp for the Chinese revolution much is owed to his capacity as an ideologue. Of his military powers there was little doubt by the end of the harrowing Long March, nor was there any doubt that he was a masterly leader of the Party. He had shed various opponents on the way – but not merely in the name of personal power; more importantly it was in the name of his vision of a recreated China, where one Chinese was equal to another Chinese and possibly more equal (but only so within the limits of socialism) than people from abroad. In brief, Mao's charisma lay very much in his power as an ideological leader. He was an active prophet, a man commanding both the gun and the theoretical essay.

But there is a problem regarding charisma, as Max Weber well recognized – and Mao seems to have seen it too. The problem is that the charisma is absorbed by functionaries and is made into a sacred routine – the charisma is routinized. This is by now a banal observation. The charismatic prophet's words are taken as authoritative, naturally, and so become the subject of commentary. The spirit leaks out in the wooden casks of comment: the prophet's desire for the permanence of his teaching issues in the establishment of an organization of his disciples or comrades to ensure the continued teaching of the doctrines. All this involves some institutionalization of the prophet's power. For these and other reasons, the prophet's breakthrough ends in a certain bureaucratization of the administration of his insights. From this point of view, the Cultural Revolution and other manifestations represent an attempt by Mao to reassert his charisma. But owing to the fact that, as we have noted, Mao's charisma owes much to his thought, the reactivation of charisma has a necessarily theoretical content. This is the significance of his idea of permanent contradiction and revolution.

To sum up: Maoism does function analogically as a religion for China. In the circumstances of China's disorientation by occidentals (if the pun may be permitted) a new spiritual force was needed. Further, the voluntarism of Mao's thought corresponds to a widespread phenomenon. When a society is functioning fairly smoothly and organically, individuals can play their various roles without any great strain. But where a society has to be put together again and in the process be changed, extra power and conformity have to be built into the individuals. Very often the evangelical spirit is the cure for insecurity and disorientation. This squares, too, with the elements of puritanism in Mao and the stress on physical toughness. Opium and gambling were symptoms and accelerators of the social chaos creeping through nineteenth-century China.

All this means that Maoism is only partially for export. In this respect it is a little like the modern Hindu ideology. Where a powerful culture claiming universal validity collides with another culture hitherto dreamily seeing itself as at the centre of things, then the second culture, to protect itself, needs a countervailing ideology which plays in the same league. In other words, the universal has to be met with the universal. So, in theory, the Hindu ideology is for export, and in the logic of things is indeed very modestly exported (by the Rama-krishna movement and others); but the main preoccupation is with the home base. So too Maoism, as a new national religion for a reconstructed China.

And when Mao is gone I suspect he will become even more sacred; for China's modern problem has been to hold itself together from the centre. Fiefs and baronies are ever likely in the variegated provinces. The ideology will become an even more important instrument of cohesion. Whether the pictures painted on the blankness of the people are beautiful remains to be seen. Despite the strains of purity and production, they will doubtless be grateful for the national dignity he has restored to them, and the freedom from their worst miseries. Maoism's meaning lies in its success.

There is a heroic socialist-realist picture of Mao after the grim battle of the Lushan pass. He stands flanked by Chou En-lai and Lin Piao. He is serene and alert, with a cigarette between his fingers. He has fire in his belly, smoke in his lungs, ice in his mind, and he is blowing hot and cold for China.

Bibliography

The quotations from Mao are nearly all from the English translation of the second Chinese edition (1960) of *Selected Works of Chairman Mao* (Peking, Foreign Languages Press, 1965).

A full bibliography of Mao's writings can be found in Jerome Ch'en *Mao Papers anthology and bibliography* (London, Oxford University Press, 1970). Also useful is Winberg Chai (ed.) *Essential Works of Chinese Communism* (New York, Bantam Matrix, 1972) – but it is not always clear where passages are omitted from the original.

Also Mao's writings are usefully excerpted in Stuart R. Schram *The Political Thought of Mao Tse-tung* (revised ed., New York, Vintage Paperbacks, 1970). The first two of the above volumes are a substantive collection of Mao's works (the Peking edition involves emendation of the originals, but such an official doctoring no doubt represents in a rough and ready way Mao's hindsight on his own work).

As for biographies, probably the fullest is Jerome Ch'en's *Mao and the Chinese Revolution* (London, Oxford University Press, 1965) which includes a translation of Mao's poems. Also, R. Payne, *Portrait of a Revolutionary: Mao Tse-tung* (New York, 1961). A brief biography is found in W. Barnstone, in collaboration with Ko Ching-po, *The Poems of Mao Tse-tung* (New York, Bantam Books, 1972) which includes the Chinese text. There is a wealth of analytic writing on Maoism, for which see the bibliographies in Jerome Ch'en and Winberg Chai above.

Notes

Chapter 5
1 Donald E. MacInnis: *Religious Policy in Communist China — a documentary history* (London, 1972), p. 16 – quoted from *Anti-Memoirs* by André Malraux.
2 N.I. Jerome Ch'en, ed.: *Mao Papers, anthology and bibliography* (London, 1970), p. 96.

Chapter 10
1 See for example my *Religious Experience of Mankind* (Collins, 1971), chapter 1.
2 Quoted in *The Poems of Mao Tse-tung*, by Willis Barnnstone and Ko Ching-Po.